I Wish
I Felt Good
All the
Time

I Wish I Felt Good All the Time

MILDRED TENGBOM

BETHANY HOUSE PUBLISHERS
MINNEAPOLIS, MINNESOTA 55438
A Division of Bethany Fellowship, Inc.

Photos by Dick Easterday and Larry Swenson.

Scripture references are taken from the *Revised Standard Version* of the Bible, unless otherwise noted.

Published by Bethany House Publishers
A Division of Bethany Fellowship, Inc.
6820 Auto Club Road, Minneapolis, Minnesota 55438

Printed in the United States of America

Library of Congress Cataloging in Publication Data

Tengbom, Mildred.
  I wish I felt good all the time.

    Summary: A collection of sixty devotions designed to help children
and parents verbalize and understand their feelings.
    1. Children—Prayer-books and devotions—English. [1. Prayer books
and devotions. 2. Communication. 3. Parent and child]
I. Title
BV4870.T43   1983   248.8'2   83-2616
ISBN 0-87123-281-2

The Author

MILDRED TENGBOM has four children of her own, two boys and two girls. She loves youngsters and thinks they all are important. She is concerned because often parents and other adults are so busy they don't take the time they should to listen and to understand children.

Mrs. Tengbom, author of *Does Anyone Care How I Feel?,* believes that Jesus can help children and grown-ups talk to each other. She hopes that through this second family devotional book, children will receive the help and encouragement that they need.

Books by Mildred Tengbom

Does Anyone Care How I Feel?
Is Your God Big Enough?
The Bonus Years
Table Prayers
Fill My Cup, Lord
No Greater Love: The Story of Clara Louise Maass
A Life to Cherish
Especially for Mother
Sometimes I Hurt
Bible Readings for Families
Help for Bereaved Parents
Help for Care-Givers of the Terminally Ill
Don't Waste Your Illness

Contents

An Open Letter

Hi, Kids!

This book is especially for you and your parents. It is written to help us understand why we sometimes feel the way we do and what we can do with our feelings.

Feelings are funny things. We can't prevent feelings from coming in on us, and sometimes we can't keep good feelings from disappearing when we wish they would stay.

Sometimes we don't know *why* we feel sad or lonely or why we feel happy and good. Other times we *know* why a certain feeling has come. Sometimes we just have to live with uncomfortable feelings. Other times we can do something so our feelings become more pleasant and easier to live with. This book is written to help us explore how we feel in certain situations, why we feel like we do, and what we can do about our feelings.

Telling someone else how we feel often helps. Some of our best friends can be members of our family: mother, father, sisters or brothers. Sometimes friends or teachers or camp counselors can help us.

This book will mean even more to you if you read it together with someone else: your mother or dad, a sister, brother, friend or teacher. Maybe your family would like to set aside one evening a week when you can read a portion from this book together and discuss it. It is important that this be unhurried time to talk and listen. Each member of the family should feel free to answer the questions honestly and directly without fear of "getting into trouble."

Other times you may want to read a special section with your parents when a particular situation arises where you wish you could tell your parents how you are feeling.

If you and your parents read this book together and put your feelings into words, it will help all of you understand each other's feelings in different situations. Parents sometimes don't know how their children feel. When they understand how their children feel, they are able to respond in a more loving and understanding way. When both parents and children begin to listen to and understand each other, they can love each other more and help each other.

It may happen, too, that you will want to read some of this book with your friends. Sometimes it seems easier—at least at first—to talk things over with a friend.

More than anything else, after you have read from this book I hope you will take time to talk to Jesus in prayer. You can tell Him everything. He understands better than anyone else. If you will tell Him all that is on your heart, you can be sure that He is listening and understanding and that Jesus will take care of everything.

If you want to write me a letter and tell me what the book has meant to you, I would be happy to hear from you. Address your letter in care of the publisher: Mrs. Mildred Tengbom, Bethany House Publishers, 6820 Auto Club Road, Minneapolis, Minnesota, 55438.

I want to add a word of thanks, too, to those young people who helped me in writing this book by sharing their feelings with me.

May Jesus bless you and give you all the help, courage and happiness you need. He loves you very much.

Mildred Tengbom

1

If You'd Look at Me, You'd Know How I Feel

"The trouble with you is you don't communicate!" Mother said.
I didn't know what "communicate" meant.
I had to ask Dad.
Dad said "communicate" means to let someone know
    what you think
    and how you feel.
I thought about that a long time
    and decided
    that really I do communicate.
Sometimes I can tell people what I think or feel
    without saying it in words.
I think if Mom would look at me carefully,
    she'd see me communicating.
But, maybe I need to talk to Mom more, too,
    instead of expecting her to read my mind.

Let's Talk

How can we communicate without talking?
Take turns and show each other how you can communicate
that you are:

sad	perplexed	confused	disappointed
happy	worried	surprised	mad
afraid	frustrated	scared	amused

How do Mom and Dad communicate to you without words?
How do they tell you they are upset? irritated? worried? frus-

11

trated? happy? disappointed? Can you show what their expressions are?

Watch carefully this next week to see how people communicate without words. Make a note of this. Next week share your observations with each other.

Read Luke 5:8. What do you think Simon Peter was communicating by his action?

Read Luke 7:37, 38. What was the woman communicating by her actions?

Read Luke 9:16. Notice all Jesus' different actions. What was He communicating by His actions?

Read Mark 10:16. What did Jesus communicate by His actions in this instance?

It Helps to Remember

There are many ways by which we tell people how we feel or what we think. We tell them by the expressions on our faces, by the posture of our bodies or our movements, by the way we use our hands, by how close we get to people, by the way we touch people, and in many other ways. What we feel inside has a way of coming through, and people can understand that too. It would help us all if we became more aware of what others are communicating without words.

Verses to Remember

The Psalmist says even nature communicates, although nature cannot use words.

"The heavens are telling the glory of God;
    and the firmament proclaims his handiwork.
Day to day pours forth speech,
    and night to night declares knowledge.
There is no speech, nor are there words;
    their voice is not heard;
yet their voice goes out through all the earth
    and their words to the ends of the world" (Ps. 19:1-4).

2

My Special Grown-up Friend

Thank you so much, Lord, for our postman.
He's my special summer friend.
I wait until I see him drive into our block.
I run to greet him.
He puts down his bag and shakes my hand with
    a friendly grin.
Then he turns off his radio
    so we can talk together.
I push his buggy for him
    with the big leather bags on each side.
We talk as we walk along.
I have to half-run because he has to keep moving
    to cover so many blocks in so many minutes,
    but he laughs
    and says his tongue can move with his legs.
He asks what I'm doing
    and what I want to be when I grow up
    and how our team's doing in baseball.
He tells me stories—
    he's a fan—tas—tic storyteller.

Yesterday I was going to be gone with Mom and the other kids to
    the beach.
It was a steaming hot day.
Before we left I filled a huge glass with lemonade and ice cubes
    and left it in the shade by our mailbox
    with a note:
        "This is for you, Mr. Postman. I know you'll be thirsty."

This morning when I ran to meet him,
    he reached into his pocket and took out
    a baseball cap and a whistle!
"This is for you," he said.
"Wow, thanks!" I said
    and blew the whistle.
It's sure great having friends who make you feel special, Lord.
Thank You for my postman friend.

Let's Talk

Can you think of some times when someone did something special for you to show that he or she loved you?

How did you feel?

When have you done something special for others?

What did they say?

Can Mom or Dad or adults in your group think of something special you did for them?

How did they feel?

What have Mom and Dad done for you that has made you feel special?

Do you know anyone who needs someone to be extra kind to him or her?

Do you have any special grown-up friends? Tell about them.

It Helps to Remember

We all need friends. Our family members can be some of our best friends, but we need friends outside of our family too.

To be a friend and to have friends we need to spend time with each other, talk with each other, and show kindness to each other.

A Verse to Remember

"Let love be genuine" (Rom. 12:9).

3

I Can't Help It That I'm Short

Dear Lord,
I hate it when the kids at school say,
    "Bob! you *really* are short!"
I can't help it that I'm short!
    Why do they always have to talk about it?
I never know what to say.
Sometimes I laugh and joke about it,
    but inside
    I'm angry and resentful
    and feel small.
What do I do with these feelings, Lord?

Let's Talk

What things about your body don't you like?

What remarks do people make about you that are embarrassing?

What do the adults in your group or family not like about themselves?

Does it make any difference to you that your mom and dad and sisters and brothers and friends aren't "perfect beauties"?

What particular things do you like about your mom and dad and sisters and brothers and friends?

What do they like about you? Go around the circle and talk about this.

What do you like about your friends?

If we want to be a real friend, what kind of remarks should we avoid making?

Read the story in Luke 19:1-10.

What do you suppose it had been like for Zacchaeus to be so short?

What do you think people had said to him?

How did Jesus begin to give Zacchaeus a sense of self-worth?

How did Zacchaeus feel when of all the people around Him Jesus chose Zacchaeus' house as the place He wanted to visit?

What wrong things had Zacchaeus done? (v. 8).

Do you suppose that doing these wrong things could have been Zacchaeus' way of getting even with people for making fun of him?

When Zacchaeus began to have a sense of self-worth and know that Jesus loved him, how did he change?

It Helps to Remember

Have you ever wondered who decided what measurements the "perfect body" should have? No two trees are exactly alike, nor do we talk about "perfect" trees and admire only those trees that have a "perfect" shape. In fact, we *want* trees to have different shapes and sizes. Shouldn't we accept different body shapes and sizes and see beauty in them?

Because our society places so much emphasis on what some people have defined as the "perfect body," all of us at one time or another wish we looked different than we do. We need to learn to look beyond outer beauty and instead look for the inner beauty of people. If we are beautiful people on the inside, that beauty will show through. Of course, how I care for myself, how I keep myself clean and neat is important. But being tall or short, having a big nose or a little one, wearing glasses or not wearing glasses, having big feet or little feet—none of these things is the most important.

A Verse to Remember

"Thou didst form my inward parts, thou didst knit me together in my mother's womb" (Ps. 139:13).

4

I Felt Like a Little Kid

I felt so strange, Lord.
Jennie, Stephanie and I were playing with our Barbie dolls
   and really having a good time.
Then Dennis came along,
   and Jennie, quick-like,

dropped her doll and said,
"Oh, *they're* playing Barbie dolls."
I felt like a little kid.
Dennis kept on standing there
    staring at us,
    so I finally scooped up the dolls
    and dumped them in a box.
"Yah, I know it's dumb," I said,
    but inside I was mad.
Jennie was playing Barbie dolls too.
Why did she have to pretend she wasn't
    and that she was too grown-up for dolls?
And *I like* to play with Barbie dolls.
Why can't I if I like to?

Let's Talk

Instead of dumping her dolls in a box, what could Sherrie have done and said?

Have you ever had someone make you feel little or immature? Explain.

Have Mom or Dad or the adults in your group ever felt this way? Ask them to tell about it. How did they handle the situation?

What can you do or say so you're not left feeling so dumb?

It Helps to Remember

All of us have different likes and dislikes. Just because my likes are different from others does not mean necessarily that I am dumb or wrong. Sherrie could have said quietly, "You may think it's 'kids' stuff' to play with Barbie dolls, but I like to. Besides, we're all still kids!"

Verses to Remember

"Love is kind. . . . Love is not arrogant or rude" (1 Cor. 13:4, 5).

5

I Did What Was Right

Today's been a miserable day, Lord.
Yesterday my three best friends went to Disneyland
    all alone
    with no supervision
    for fifteen whole hours.
They lied to their parents.
    Each one said one of the other mothers was going along
    but no one really was.
They wanted me to go too,
    but I wouldn't.
In the first place, I knew
    Mom would find out
    we were unsupervised.
    She always does.
And I didn't feel right about being there
    fifteen whole hours
    without an adult.
I felt good about my decision.
But today these friends of mine
    called me
    six, seven times
    from a pay phone.
"Why didn't you come?" they taunted.
"You're chicken," they cackled into the phone.
They make me feel like dirt,
    and I hate it!

Let's Talk

Before they went to Disneyland, what two wrong things were
the friends asking Paul to do?

Why do you think the friends kept on bugging Paul about his decision not to go?

Have you ever had someone make fun of you because you wouldn't do something that he or she wanted you to do?

How did you feel?

Has Mom or Dad ever had this happen to them? Ask them to tell about it.

How could Paul have handled all the phone calls that came?

It Helps to Remember

Temptations to do wrong will come. When we refuse to do wrong, sometimes people will make fun of us in order to deaden their own guilty feelings. We can say, "I did what I believe was right, and I am glad I did."

Verses to Remember

"Many others have faced exactly the same problems before you. And no temptation is irresistible. You can trust God to keep the temptation from becoming so strong that you can't stand up against it, for he has promised this and will do what he says. He will show you how to escape temptation's power so that you can bear up patiently against it" (1 Cor 10:13, 14, TLB).

6

Getting Even

Getting even doesn't work—
    at least not for me, Lord.
There are three of us who are best friends,
    Susie, Denise and me.
I don't know why, but Susie is always saying or doing things
    to make people feel bad.
She does it to Denise and me too,
    so we decided to get even with her
    and show her what it's like.
We said all kinds of mean things
    and looked at her strange
    and walked away from her
    and hid her bike.
It worked.
She stopped talking bad to us
    and treated us very nice so we'd stop being mean to her.
But I felt so bad about it all inside, Lord.
Finally I called her
    and talked for two hours
    and told her "I'm sorry."
She said, "Okay."
But now she's back to her old ways of hurting people.
I feel bad about that,
    but one thing I know for sure, Lord.
I can't behave like that again
    to make *her* feel bad.

Let's Talk

Why did Sherrie feel bad because of the way she treated Susie?

Why couldn't she feel good about this even though it worked?

Have you ever joined your friends in doing something you shouldn't have and then afterward felt bad?

If you tell your friends you are sorry you did what you did, how do they respond?

Have they ever laughed at you or told you it's dumb for you to feel sorry about what you did?

How does that make you feel?

Instead of our trying to get even with those who mistreat us, what is a better thing to do?

Discuss the verses below.

It Helps to Remember

When someone we love says or does something that hurts others, we can try to make up for it. We can say, "I don't think Susie meant it like it sounded. I know she thinks you are really pretty." Or we can smile and put our arm around the one who has been hurt. And we can keep on praying that Jesus will change Susie. Often when people are unkind to others it is because *they* are unhappy. We can think about this and see if we can discover *why* they are unhappy. Then we can do what we can to make them happy. Happy, contented people rarely are unkind.

Verses to Remember

"Dear friends, never avenge yourselves. Leave that to God, for he has said that he will repay those who deserve it . . . conquer evil by doing good" (Rom. 12:19, 21, TLB).

7

Our Nosey Neighbor

Lord, that nosey neighbor of ours bugs me!
I mean old Mr. Smith.
He's always outside when I come home from school.
"How'd it go today?" he asks.
"Fine," I say, hurrying toward the door.
"Any tests? What grades did you get?"
"No tests," I say, even if we had one.
I wish he didn't make me lie!
What business is it of his what grades I get?
"Sure's a pretty little girl next door."
I feel like I'm going to bust, I'm so mad.
I don't say anything.
"Work goin' all right for your dad?
    He looks kind of worried these days.
    Or is something else bothering him?"
I know he's hinting about Mom and Dad,
    but just because they disagree once in a while
    doesn't mean they're not going to stay married.
"Everybody is worried about the economy," I say,
    remembering that this is what I hear the grown-ups
       talking about lots.
He's so surprised at my answer that for a minute
    my nosey neighbor doesn't say a thing.
He just stares at me.
"I gotta do some chores," I say
    and dive through the door.
I know I shouldn't feel this way,
But I can't stand that nosey old man, Lord.
How'll I get by him tomorrow?

Let's Talk

Do you know someone who is always prying into your private affairs?

How does this make you feel?

Have Mom or Dad or the adults in your group had this experience? How do they feel and how do they handle it?

Why do you think some people want to talk every time they see you?

How can you stop disliking someone who bugs you?

It Helps to Remember

Sometimes people want to talk to us because they are lonely. They won't feel so lonely if we take a few minutes to talk with them. We can steer the conversation other directions and after a few minutes we can politely say, "I have to go now. We'll talk some more tomorrow."

A Verse to Remember

"Let no one seek his own good, but the good of his neighbor" (1 Cor. 10:24).

8

Fears

Dear Lord,
Please bless my new friend, Felicia.
She needs Your help.
I guess I've learned to know Felicia better than
    most kids in our class know her.
English is Felicia's second language,
    and she's afraid to say much
        because she's afraid if she makes a mistake,
        the other kids will laugh.
I asked her to stay overnight with me last night,
    and discovered she is scared of lots of things.
She's afraid of the dark;
    we had to leave the light on all night.
She's afraid of sleeping alone in a room.
She's afraid of thunderstorms,
    and dogs,
    and the principal at our school—
    she's heard he shouts at kids.
She's afraid of airplanes
    and drowning
    and robbers
    and hospitals
    and doctors
    and dentists.
She's afraid to go some place alone
    because she's afraid she will get lost.
She has so many fears, Lord.
It can't be good for her to be this afraid all the time.
I wish I could help her,
    but I don't know what to do.
Dear Lord, can You teach me how to be a good friend to her?

And please take care of her fears.
She doesn't know You.
I feel if she knew You that would help too.
Please, Jesus, help me to tell Felicia about You,
    and help her to understand how much You love her.

Let's Talk

Do you know anyone who is fearful much of the time?

When others talk to you about their fears, how do you feel?

How do you think they feel when they are afraid so much of the time?

What can we do to help people who are full of fears?

Read Matthew 14:22-33. What did the disciples fear? What did Jesus do?

It Helps to Remember

All of us have some fears from time to time. But if we have many fears all of the time, we need the help a wise adult can give us.

Verses to Remember

"God is our refuge and strength,
    a very present help in trouble.
Therefore we will not fear
    though the earth should change" (Ps. 46:1, 2).

9

Slow Learner

I feel so terrible, Lord,
    I wish I were dead.
Mom sometimes reminds me about how slow I am.
"You were slow getting toilet-trained," she begins,
    "and slow feeding yourself,
    and slow talking
    and slow walking.
You were slow learning how to make your bed right,
    and look at it now."
She goes on and on, Lord.
I know I'm not perfect,
    and maybe I'm a year or two behind some others,
    but maybe I just grow slower or something.
I try.
I just don't succeed good enough to make Mom happy.
Grandma doesn't mind.
She hugs me and says, "Be patient, now."
I guess she thinks I'll catch up in time.
I wonder,
    do You think I will, Lord?

Let's Talk

Does anyone ever expect you to do more or do better than you
do?

What do they say?

How do you feel then?

Ask Mom or Dad or the adults in your group if anybody ever
made them feel dumb. Did they have older brothers or sisters
who told them to "grow up"?

How can you answer people who ask you, "Why don't you grow up?"

Might there be times when you *could* "grow up," but you don't want to? Can you think of examples?

What may be some reasons why you don't want to grow up?

It Helps to Remember

We learn to do more and more things well as we get older and grow bigger. Some of us grow more slowly and for some of us it takes longer to learn than it takes others. We can say, "Be patient with me. Give me time." Also, we can put special effort into doing those things that people say we should do in order to "grow up."

A Verse to Remember

"For everything there is a season
and a time for every matter under heaven" (Eccles. 3:1).

10

Bringing My Friends Home for Dinner

We had just finished our ball game.
"Have to get home," I said.
    "It's time for our dinner."
"You're lucky," Phil said.
    "Our dad doesn't live with Tom and me anymore.
    Just Mom.
    And Mom works till eight.
    She usually puts something in the fridge for us
        to warm in the microwave,
        but it's no fun sitting there and eating all alone."
"Why don't you come home with me?" I invited.
"I smelled a roast in the oven before I left,
    and there were two pies on the counter top."
"Wow!" Phil and Tom said in one breath.
Their noses twitched
    and even their eyes looked hungry.
"Sure, come along!" I repeated.
"Mom," I called as we stepped into the kitchen,
    "I've brought Phil and Tom for dinner.
    I knew you wouldn't mind."
And then I saw the dining room table all set up real pretty
    with flowers and candles.
Mom bit her lip and looked uncertain.
Phil and Tom hung their heads and edged toward the door,
    but I saw their hungry eyes on the pies.
"They can have my pie," I said,
    "and we can sit in the kitchen."
Just then Dad walked in.

Dad understands things like this real quick.

"You fellows look hungry enough to eat a whole cow,"
    he said.

"I don't think we could fill up both you and our guests. . . . But
    I know!" He dug in his pocket.

    "How about going out for pizza tonight,
        and then come back tomorrow
        and we'll have pie?"

Wow, Lord!

I let out a long, low whistle.

Pizza is Phil and Tom's favorite,
    and I mean *favorite.*

How'd Dad know?

And tomorrow we get pie.

O Lord, I'm so glad I can share my lucky home with Phil and
Tom.

Let's Talk

Have you ever invited friends home for a meal before you
checked with your mom and dad?

Ask your mom or dad how they feel when this happens.

How do you feel when you want your friends to eat with you
and your mother says no?

Does Dad sometimes wish he could invite his friends but
doesn't because of the work it will cause Mom?

What are some of the different ways this problem can be
solved?

It Helps to Remember

Being a family involves work. Rooms have to be cleaned,
meals cooked, laundry and shopping done, yard work and cars
fixed, etc. Work should be shared by all members of the family.
Opening our homes to others can be a fun experience, but the extra work involved in doing so should be shared by all.

Verses to Remember

"Practice hospitality ungrudgingly to one another" (1 Pet. 4:9).

"Everyone must make up his own mind as to how much he should give. Don't force anyone to give more than he really wants to, for cheerful givers are the ones God prizes" (2 Cor. 9:8, TLB).

11

Secret Stuff

Whew! I caught it just in time!
For our English class I had written an essay
    that was really personal.
We weren't going to read our essays aloud in class,
    and I like my teacher,
      so I went ahead and wrote my heart out.
But guess what happened?
Tonight is Open House for PTA,
    and there on the bulletin board
    for everyone to read
    was my essay!
Lucky for me none of the kids had seen it.
I went to my teacher
    and explained how I felt,
    and she took it down right away.
Wow, Lord! A person never knows what grown-ups
    are going to do next.
I sure wish they'd think to ask us first.

Let's Talk

Have you ever had anything like that happen to you?
How did you feel?
What did you do?

Have Mom or Dad ever had any of their private matters made public? Have Mom or Dad ever heard others make remarks about them publicly that have embarrassed them? How did they feel?

Does anyone snoop in your drawers or read your letters?
How does this make you feel?

Do you ever hear grown-ups talking about you and telling something that embarrasses you? Tell about it.

What can you do to prevent this happening again?

When children tell family matters to their friends and this gets back to parents, how do parents feel?

If we don't want others to read something written, what should we do with it?

It Helps to Remember

We all have a right to privacy. Families have family secrets that shouldn't be told to others.

A Verse to Remember

"He who goes about as a talebearer
   reveals secrets,
  but he who is trustworthy in
    spirit keeps a thing hidden" (Prov. 11:13).

12

Mom's Scissors

Mom sighed again today, Lord.
    "I can never find my scissors when I need them."
I had them, Lord.
When Mom wasn't looking
    I sneaked them back in her drawer.
If I'd told her I had them,
    she would have said,
    "Why are you always taking mine?
    I gave you a pair of your own."
I know she did,
    but I can never find mine.
Why does she have to complain about not finding her old scissors?
Don't we all live together in this house?
Shouldn't we let the whole family use our stuff, even if they don't
    ask?

Let's Talk

Does anyone ever use your things without asking?
How do you feel about this?
What do you think about the question: "Shouldn't we let the whole family use our stuff, even if they don't ask?" Do you agree with that?
Read 2 Samuel 12:1-6. What does this parable teach us about ownership and taking the things of others without permission?

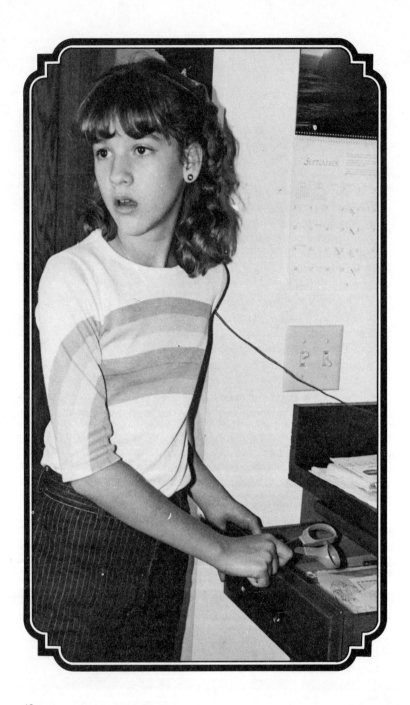

It Helps to Remember

In the instance of the parable of the Rich Man, the rich man's sin was very serious because he actually destroyed the little pet lamb of the poor man. In most cases we only borrow things that belong to others with the intention of using them for only a short while. But even then, when we do so without permission, it is wrong. We each have a right to own certain things. We need to respect this right of others also and not use their things without their consent. And as owners we need to learn how to care properly for our things. If someone asks to use something of ours and we know they are careless, we can refuse politely and say, "I really don't think I'd better loan out my bike." We also should learn to put away our things so they aren't lying out, handy and easy for others to use.

A Verse to Remember

"Let no one despise your youth, but set the believers an example in speech and conduct, in love, in faith, in purity" (1 Tim. 4:12).

13

Sometimes I Want to Be Alone

Grandpa died, Lord.
He wasn't sick at all;
    he was just old.
But he had been old as long as I can remember.
Mom said his heart got tired
    and stopped working.
It seemed so strange!
We went miniature golfing just the day before he died.
After we finished playing,

we stopped for hamburgers.
I felt so funny last night when I saw him lying in the coffin.
They hadn't combed his hair right,
    and he had his eyes closed like he was sleeping,
    but he had his glasses on.
He really wasn't sleeping.
He just wasn't there.
He looked like Grandpa,
    and yet he didn't look like Grandpa.
I felt so funny.
When we got home
    I came here to my room
    and lay on my bed and looked at the ceiling.
Mom came in
    and wanted to hug me and talk.
I rolled over and faced the wall.
    "I'd rather not talk," I said. "Can you please leave me
    alone?"
Why can't parents understand
    that sometimes we just want to be quiet?

Let's Talk

Has a grandparent or relative or friend of yours ever died?
Who? How did you feel?
What did you do?
What did your parents do or say?
Did it help?
Why do we sometimes want to be alone? Ask those in your group to explain when they like to be alone and why.
Is it hard for them to find a place and time to be alone?
When does talking help us and how does it help?

It Helps to Remember

We feel bad when someone we love dies. Often we feel confused, too, and have questions. As we sort out things and move on to feeling better, we need both to be with others and to be alone.

To have a happy family or to be a good friend we need to respect each other's need to be alone, but we also need to be ready to spend time with and listen to each other when that is needed.

Verses to Remember

"My mouth praises thee with joyful lips
when I think of thee upon my bed,
     and meditate on thee in the watches of the night;
for thou hast been my help,
     and in the shadow of thy wings I sing for joy.
My soul clings to thee;
     thy right hand upholds me" (Ps. 63:5-8).

14

How Can I Know God Has Forgiven Me?

Becky, Rachel, April and I
    were lying on our backs watching the clouds float by.
"I wonder what it's like to die," Becky said.
"I hope I go to heaven," Rachel said.
"How can we be sure
    we will go to heaven?" Becky asked,
    rolling over and propping herself up on her elbows.
"My dad says all we can do
    is be as good as we can
    and hope for the best," Rachel said.
"I don't think that will work," Becky said.
    "Even when I try really hard
    to be good,
    I can't.
    Not for long, that is.
    I might get through two, three hours,
    but that's about all—"
"My dad says," April interrupted,
    "that we won't get to heaven
    by trying to be good.
    He says no way could we ever be good enough.
    He says that God understood this,
    and so He sent His Son to die for us.
        Jesus took the punishment that should be ours
        and because of that, we can be forgiven for all the bad
        things we do."
"My dad says," I chimed in,
    "that God wanted us to know how much He loves us
    and so He sent His Son, Jesus.
Jesus taught us about God
    and Jesus showed us what God is like,

45

but most of all,
Jesus proved how great God's love for us is
by dying for us.
When we understand how much God loves us,
we want to love Him in return."
"I love Jesus," Becky said seriously.
"I really want to follow Him,
and I'm thankful Jesus died for me."

Let's Talk

Have you ever wondered if God has forgiven you for all the wrong things you've done?

Read 1 John 1:9. What does this verse say we should do? What does this verse say God will do?

What more does God promise to do according to Isaiah 43:25?

Why is God willing to forgive us? Read John 3:16 and Romans 5:6.

Have you ever thanked God for loving you enough to send Jesus to die for you? Have you ever thanked Him for making you His child? Have you ever thanked Him for forgiving you?

Spend a little time in prayer as a family or friends thanking God for all these things.

It Helps to Remember

God loves us and forgives us, not because we deserve it nor because of anything we do, but simply because He loves us. He loves us so much He was willing to send His only Son, Jesus, to die for us. He sent the Holy Spirit to help us understand these spiritual truths and believe in Jesus. It's a good feeling to know that we are God's forgiven children, loved by Him. He will never, never give up on us.

Verses to Remember

"I will forgive their iniquity, and I will remember their sin no more" (Jer. 31:34).

"Thou wilt cast all our sins into the depths of the sea" (Mic. 7:19).

15

Should Children Go to Funerals?

Julie's grandma died.
We all feel so sad.
She was the neatest lady,
    always happy
    and full of smiles and laughter.
We thought she'd gotten over her cancer,
    and everybody was feeling good about that.
But it came back,
    and when it did,
    the doctors shook their heads
    and said there wasn't anything they could do.
I didn't know she had died, though,
    until this morning
    when I stopped at Julie's house
    on the way to school.
Julie was crying *so hard*.
I thought about her all day.
After school I knew I should see her again,
    but I felt awkward about going
    and wondered what I should say.
Julie wasn't crying when I came,
    but she wanted to talk.
She said she wanted to go to the funeral,
    but her mom said
    it would be better to remember Grandma
        as she was when she was alive.
Julie asked me what I thought she should do.
I didn't know what to say,
    and I still don't know, Lord.
What do You think is best?

Let's Talk

Ask everybody in the family to draw a picture to show what they think death is like. Compare each other's pictures and explain their meaning.

Have you ever gone to a funeral? Tell about it if you have.

How do funeral directors prepare a body for a funeral? Ask Mom and Dad to explain this to you.

If you haven't been at a funeral, have them tell you what a funeral is like.

Can they think of a funeral service that helped them and brought them comfort?

Do you feel awkward talking to someone whose relative or close friend has died?

Why do you think you feel this way?

What can we do or say that is helpful?

It Helps to Remember

Death of our physical body takes place when our lungs stop breathing and the heart stops pumping blood. The other body functions stop little by little. But we are not only bodies. We are persons with souls. As Christians we believe that when our bodies die, our souls go to be with God and He takes care of us. At the final resurrection day we shall be given new bodies that will be different from these bodies and perfect in every way. We also will be new people not wanting to do anything wrong but wanting only to please God.

But because we are both spirit and body, when we look at a dead body in a casket we may feel that the real person isn't there, and in one sense that is true.

However, some people say it helps them really believe the person has died when they can see the dead body. Others say the dead person looks so peaceful they feel good. Still others don't care to look at dead people.

We are all different, and there is no one answer that is right for all of us.

When people are sad after someone dies, we shouldn't stay away from them even if we feel a little uncomfortable about going to them. All we need to do is hug them and say, "I'm sorry," and if they want to talk, we can listen.

Verses to Remember

"In Christ shall all be made alive" (1 Cor. 15:22).

(Other verses to read and discuss are: Rom. 14:7-8; John 11:25-26; 12:23-26; 1 Cor. 15:51-57; Phil. 3:20-21.)

16

If We Didn't Like the Same Things, We Wouldn't Fight So Much

Some kids have problems
    because they're so different from each other.
They like different foods
    and want to go to different places
    and play different games.
But Sarah and I have another problem.
Our problem is we're both alike.
We choose the same records.
We like the same flavor ice cream.

We buy the same kinds of clothes.
Lord, what makes it tough is when we both want the same thing
    at the same time,
    and we're both stubborn about it.
When that happens
    we begin to fight.
Sometimes I think we fight too much.
We wonder about how much we fight.
Afterward we feel bad.
When we're fighting
    we're angry at each other.
Afterward we're angry at ourselves.

Let's Talk

Do you fight with your sisters and brothers because you like the same things or want the same things? Give some examples.

After your fight, how do you feel?

How would you solve the following problems?

1. Dad is going on a trip. A special offer of the airlines will allow Dad to take one child along free. Both you and your brother want to go. How can this be solved?

2. Mrs. Rossetti calls and wants a baby-sitter. Both you and your sister want to go because both of you want to earn a little extra money. How can this be decided?

3. Mother needs help cleaning the house. Both you and your brother want to do the vacuuming. Neither of you wants to dust the house or clean the bathroom. What can be done?

It Helps to Remember

Usually problems can be solved by discussing and considering different solutions. Even then, sometimes one person has to "give in" and be a peacemaker. It isn't good, however, if the same person always has to be the peacemaker. That responsibility should be shared.

When disagreements are settled by discussions rather than by angry words, people do not have to feel angry with themselves later. Instead, they have a good feeling of accomplishment.

A Verse to Remember

"Blessed are the peacemakers, for they shall be called sons of God" (Matt. 5:9).

17

It's Not Fair That Adam Gets More Than I Do

I've had it!
Adam got new jeans,
    and I didn't!
I don't know why,
    but Mom and Dad seem to love him more than they love me.
He gets to stay up late Friday nights,
    and go horseback riding on Saturdays.
He's got tons more friends than I have,
    and Mom lets him drag them all home.
He doesn't have to do as much work as I do,
    and he gets to go more places,
    and gets a bigger allowance.
It's not fair, Lord!

Let's Talk

When you think you are not being treated fairly, how do you feel?

How do you react?

What would happen if you gently asked some questions? You might ask your parents to explain why the other person gets more things or more privileges than you.

Read the paragraph on the next page and the Bible verse. Discuss the Bible verse. What do you think it means?

Pray that your family may have this kind of wisdom.

Now, is there something you would like your parents to explain to you?

Do they ever have unfair things happen to them?

It Helps to Remember

We become jealous when we feel that our parents are treating us unfairly. Sometimes parents don't realize what they have done. Discussing the problem might help them to see their mistake. Sometimes if we hear their explanation, we realize they have been fair. If we can ask questions without being afraid, knowing our parents will answer gently and with understanding, our homes will be happy.

And once in a while we may need someone else to help us to ask some questions.

A Verse to Remember

"The wisdom from above is first pure, then peaceable, gentle, open to reason, full of mercy and good fruits, without uncertainty or insincerity" (James 3:17).

18

Doing Good and Feeling Bad

So many things make me feel different
    from all the other kids, Lord.
If I like our teacher,
    and none of the other kids do,
    and I say I like our teacher,
        I feel different.
If I write a story
    and others who can't write as well say,
    "What a brain!"
        I feel different.
If I get good grades because I study
    while others fool around
    and get C's and D's,
    they say, "You're the teacher's pet,"
        and I feel different.
If I wear just plain old jeans and a top
    while others wear Jordache
    or whatever is "in,"
    they ignore me
        and I feel different.
I don't like feeling different, Lord.
At the same time I know I wouldn't be happy
    following the kids
    just for the sake of following them.
So I guess I'll just have to learn to live with
    the funny feelings that come
    when I feel different, huh?

Let's Talk

What makes you feel different?

Do Mom and Dad or the adults in your group ever feel different? Ask them to tell you about it.

Does feeling different make us feel worthwhile or do we feel small?

What do we do with these feelings?

What is best to allow to control us: feelings or convictions? Is there a difference?

Read Daniel 6. Picture yourself as Daniel. If you have time, act out the story.

How was Daniel different?

The passage doesn't tell us how Daniel felt, but use your imagination and try to imagine how he felt. Discuss this.

Did Daniel's feelings change his actions?

Daniel knew the difference between right and wrong in his situation.

Where do we get guidelines or directions to understand what is right and what is wrong?

It Helps to Remember

Some people tell us, "If you feel good, it must be all right." That might not be true. Sometimes when we do what we know is right, we may be the only one taking that stand. Others may make remarks or may even make fun of us. This may give us funny, uncomfortable feelings. It may make us feel extremely embarrassed. But we have to learn not to pay attention to those feelings but instead stick to what we believe is right. We try to be true to what we think Jesus wants us to believe, say or do. The Bible is our guide-book, just as it was Daniel's.

A Verse to Remember

"Don't copy the behavior and customs of this world, but be a new and different person with a fresh newness in all you do and think" (Rom. 12:2, TLB).

19

Why Am I Miserable After I Quarrel?

I'm sorry, Jesus.
After I've quarreled with someone,
   I feel so awful,
      and I know I need to ask Your forgiveness.
I didn't mean to fight with Jason today.
It's just that tonight
   the Oscars were on TV,
      and I really wanted to watch the show.
Jason was in the family room
   and wouldn't leave.
"No way!" he said. "I was here first
   and I'm not budging."
I got so mad, Lord.
I grabbed his notebook and papers
   and threw them all over the room.
We had a big fight,
   and Mom sent both of us to our rooms.
I feel so awful, Lord.
Why do I feel so awful when I fight?

Let's Talk

   Whom do you fight with?
   What do you fight about?
   How do you feel afterward?
   Why do you think you feel the way you do?
   What can be done to avoid fights?

Role play the fight between Jason and his sister. Ask your dad to be Jason and your mom to be the sister. You be either the father or the mother. You are in the kitchen when the fight begins. What will you do?

What makes us unwilling to give in to others?

What makes it hard for us to ask forgiveness?

What can we do about this?

How do Mom and Dad feel when we fight?

It Helps to Remember

Fighting is always wrong. It is the poorest way to settle a disagreement and really doesn't settle it. Discussion and figuring out an answer that will be acceptable to all is so much better.

If we fight, angry, hurting words are usually said and later we need to ask forgiveness.

Why do we fight? We fight and are unwilling to forgive each other because our hearts are selfish—we are interested mainly in ourselves. If we stop to ask God's help, He will change our hearts and give us an attitude that is willing to cooperate with other viewpoints. He will also help us to forgive.

Verses to Remember

"What is causing the quarrels and fights among you? Isn't it because there is a whole army of evil desires within you? You want what you don't have, so you kill to get it. You long for what others have, and can't afford it, so you start a fight to take it away from them. And yet the reason you don't have what you want is that you don't ask God for it. And even when you do ask you don't get it because your whole aim is wrong—you want only what will give you pleasure" (James 4:1-3, TLB).

"Create in me a clean heart, O God,
    and put a new and right spirit within me" (Ps. 51:10).

"If possible, so far as it depends on you, live peaceably with all" (Rom. 12:18).

20

Don't Hit Me!

Lord, I can't take it when my big brother punches me
    or pushes me around.
It hurts.
He's so much bigger and stronger than I am.
I'll bet he doesn't know how much it hurts.
He has no right
    to be mean to me, does he, Lord?
My body belongs to me,
    and I don't want anybody pushing it around
    or hurting me.
But how can I get him to stop?

Let's Talk

Have you ever had anyone punch you or pull your hair or push you?

How do you feel when this happens?

Have you ever hit anyone?

How did you feel afterward?

Have you ever gotten so angry at someone who is bullying you that you have gone after him or her and actually won? What happened? What was the final outcome?

What can you do if someone mistreats you?

Why do people attack each other physically?

If people pick on others all the time, what can we do to help the bullies and the ones they attack?

It Helps to Remember

Often when people physically attack others, they do it because they're upset or angry about something else. If someone happens to annoy them, even in a small way, they explode. We can stay away from those who are bigger than us, those who make a practice of being nasty and mean to others.

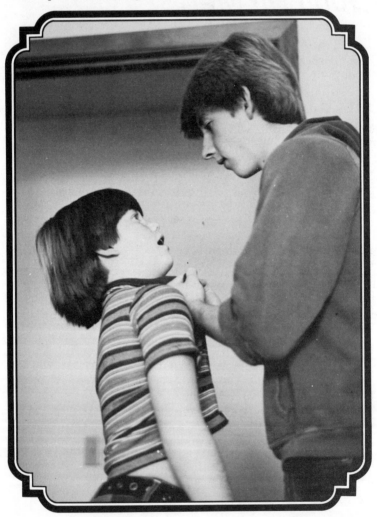

Sometimes it may be good to respond firmly and courageously when others are mean; this works especially well if you are standing up for someone else. "You may not do that to Jeffrey; I will get help if I can't stop you myself." Grabbing a bully's arm and holding tight will often work.

If we know someone who is being mistreated at home, we should tell our parents or a teacher about it.

Getting angry at someone who is mean is a natural response to the pain and hurt. But if we hold that anger inside us, it will grow into bitterness and become a sin against God. If you are not able to stop a bully, your next response should be to forgive— even if this person doesn't really deserve it. Jesus loved and forgave His enemies, and He will help us to do the same.

Verses to Remember

"Be angry, but do not sin; do not let the sun go down on your anger, and give no opportunity to the devil" (Eph. 4:26, 27).

21

When School Gets Really Tough

I feel so low, Lord.
My teacher can't understand
    why I can't solve my math problems.
"I've explained it to you before," she says.
    "Why don't you listen?"
Then she tries again,
    and I still don't get it.
I'm trying my best,
    but she thinks I'm not trying at all.
I feel so small.
Everybody else is busy
    working their problems
    and getting them,
    and I'm stuck on problem No. 1.
"Why don't you get it?" Nancy asks.
"It's really easy," Don says.
I want to say,
    "I'm trying my hardest,"
    but I don't dare.
It would help if my teacher would say,
    "I know you're trying hard.
    I have trouble, too, learning some things.
    Work on it at home tonight.
    If you still don't understand tomorrow,
        we'll try again."
At least I wouldn't feel so low,
    and I wouldn't feel like giving up.

Let's Talk

Are there certain things in school that are hard for you to learn?

Why do you think it is difficult?

What is easy to learn and do?

Have your mother and father talked with your teacher if you are having difficulties?

What is easy for your father and mother to do?

What is difficult?

What do they do when they are asked to do something difficult?

It Helps to Remember

All of us vary in what we can do well. Just because there are certain things we do not do well does not mean we are not worthwhile people. God has made all of us different and given us different gifts.

Sometimes we're just not old enough to do the things we're trying to do. It might be best for us to go back a year in school to the level we understand.

If we have extreme difficulty learning, sometimes a doctor or a trained teacher can help find out why. Some people's brain will reverse words so "was" becomes "saw." There are other learning disabilities too. When we discover what they are, we can get help.

A Verse to Remember

"Call upon me in the day of trouble;
I will deliver you, and you shall glorify me" (Ps. 50:15).

22

We Won!

I'm so excited, Lord.
We won the soccer game!
This has to be one of the happiest days in my life.
The team we played against
    creamed us before.
Not only that, but they were famous
    for trying to trip us intentionally.
But this time we tied it up
    and went into overtime.
The coach called time out,
    and put me in the goalie's place.
I was so excited, Lord,
    my heart was thumping.
Mom and Dad were on the sidelines
    yelling
    and cheering
    and telling me to play it cool
    but give it all I had,
    and we won, Lord,
    we scored and won!
I felt so good!
The first year we played we were at the bottom.
Last year we crept up to third.
And this year we won, Lord, we won!

Let's Talk

Do you play on any team or take part in contests?
Have you ever lost?
How did you feel?

If you feel sad when you lose, why is that so?

Why do you feel good when you win?

Ask Mom and Dad to tell about times when they lost and times when they won.

When is competition bad?

When is competition good?

Discuss the Bible verses under "Verses to Remember."

It Helps to Remember

Games are good for the exercise we get, the skills we develop, the friends we make, the teamwork we learn, and for the self-confidence we can develop. Games also teach us the values of winning and losing. There are so many different games that it should be possible for all of us to find some game we enjoy playing.

Verses to Remember

"Do you not know that in a race all runners compete, but only one receives the prize? So run that you may obtain it. Every athlete exercises self-control in all things" (1 Cor. 9:24, 25).

23

When It Storms

Last night it stormed.
I stood at the window and watched
    the wind bend over the tall eucalyptus trees
    until their branches swept the ground
    like a huge broom
    while the pines swayed together
    and sighed deep sighs,
    and I thought it was like a huge orchestra
    with God directing.
And then the rain came,
    just patter, patter to begin with,
    and then it poured
    until sheets of water poured down so fast
    the ground couldn't soak it all up,
    and after a while
    it looked as though our house
    was Noah's ark
    on an ocean of water.
But when lightning cut across the sky,
    I'd cringe
    and shut my eyes
    and plug my ears,
    especially
    when the thunder went crash! bang! clap!
But then I'd
    put my face to the window again
    to stare at all the force and power and fury
    twirling around outside.
When the rain slacked off
    and finally stopped altogether,
    and the trees stood just shivering and quivering
        and soaking wet,
    and the thunder faded to a distant rumble,

Dad came in
and asked me to sit by him on the couch.
Then he took out a book and began to read
about how God created the world.
And the words
made pictures
and created sounds
and filled my heart.

Let's Talk

How do you feel when it storms?
How do Mom and Dad feel?
Ask your mom or dad to get the book *God's Trombones* from the library. It is written by James Weldon Johnson. Ask them to read "Creation" to you. Maybe you'll even want to memorize it as a family.

It Helps to Remember

Our God is great and mighty and powerful, much greater than we can ever imagine. Even though it is sometimes hard to believe and understand this, still He is in control of everything. It is good for us to feel a sense of awe and wonder when we think how great God is.

Verses to Remember

"O Lord, our Lord,
how majestic is thy name in all the earth!
Thou whose glory above the heavens is chanted
    by the mouth of babes and infants. . . .
When I look at thy heavens, the work of thy fingers,
    the moon and the stars which thou hast established;
what is man that thou art mindful of him,
    and the son of man that thou dost care for him?
Yet thou hast made him little less than God,
    and dost crown him with glory and honor. . . .
O Lord, our Lord,
    how majestic is thy name in all the earth!" (Ps. 8:1-5, 9).

24

I Didn't Mean to Hurt Mom

I feel so terrible, Lord.
    I hurt Mom.
I didn't mean to hurt her.
In fact, I wasn't even thinking about Mom
    when I went home with Paula after school today.

I was just thinking about Paula and me.
We started playing a game,
    and before I knew it,
    it was 5 o'clock.
Whew!
I flew home
    but Mom already had come home from work.
"Where've you been?" she asked as I came in the door.
    Her voice was sharp.
    It hardly ever is.
    "I've been so worried!"
I explained.
"But you know you're supposed to call me
    if you don't come directly home from school."
"I know, I know.
    I didn't mean to stay at Paula's so long."
"Your bed's not made."
Whoops! I'd forgotten.
I left the house in such a hurry this morning
    I didn't get it made.
I thought I'd make it as soon as I got home
    before Mom got home and saw it.
"I'm sorry!" I said,
    and then I saw tears in her eyes.
That made me feel really bad.
I'd never realized before that when I disobey Mom I hurt her.
I don't like to hurt my mom, Lord.
She's so good to me and loves me so much.
I'm sorry I was so thoughtless, Lord.
Help me to think more carefully next time, won't You?
Please, Lord.

Let's Talk

Do you sometimes hurt your mom and dad? How? By doing what?

How do you feel when you do something that hurts your mom or dad?

Why do you think you feel this way?

What is the best thing to do after this happens?
How do you feel then?
Ask Mom and Dad how they feel when you disobey them.
Why do they feel this way?
How do they express their feelings?
Ask Mom and Dad if they have realized how bad you feel when you hurt them.
If they realize this, what might this help them do?
What is the difference between accidentally doing what is wrong and deliberately doing something that is wrong?

It Helps to Remember

We feel bad when we hurt people we love because we love them very much. If we didn't love them, we wouldn't feel so bad. So, too, we feel unhappy when we sin because we know we have hurt Jesus, and we love Him very much. It's good that we feel unhappy. We should feel unhappy when we've done wrong. Feeling unhappy will help prevent us from continuing to do wrong.

Verses to Remember

"Now I am glad I sent it . . . because the pain turned you to God. It was a good kind of sorrow you felt, the kind of sorrow God wants his people to have. . . . For God sometimes uses sorrow in our lives to help us turn away from sin and seek eternal life. . . . Just see how much good this grief from the Lord did for you! You no longer shrugged your shoulders, but became earnest and sincere, and very anxious to get rid of the sin that I wrote you about. . . . You went right to work on the problem and cleared it up. . . . How happy this makes me" (2 Cor. 7:9, 10, 11, 16, TLB).

25

It's Not Fair to Force Me!

Wow, Lord, when I said I'd join the secret club at school,
 I didn't know what I was getting into!
"We meet at Derrick's house," the guys said,
 after I said I'd join.
"Only club members know this,
 so don't tell anyone,
 not even your folks."
"But I always have to tell my mother where I am
 if I don't come home after school," I said.
"Oh, no, you don't. You don't tell her about this.
 Tell her you're staying to play basketball or something.
 This is a secret!"
So I lied to Mom this morning,
 and You know how miserable I felt all day, Lord.
But I was shivery excited about meeting with the gang too.
Derrick's mom and dad don't come home till late.
 so we had the garage all to ourselves.
I don't think Derrick's mom and dad care much what he does.
He had the garage fixed up all weird
 with black cloth over the ceiling
 and weird pictures on the wall
 and a stereo blasting.
The boys pricked my finger and made me dip my pen in blood
 and sign my name on a sheet.
I thought it was a joke.
Then they gave me a cigarette to smoke
 and a can of beer to drink.
It was part of the initiation ceremony.
Then I saw another guy
 holding a needle behind his back
 and I knew I was in trouble, Lord,

real trouble. The joke was over.
"Go ahead, what're you waiting for?" the fellows asked.
"Chicken?"
"Yellow?"
"Fraidy cat?"
And they started to laugh.
"I just don't want to," I said.
   "I don't believe in smoking or drinking.
   I will never use drugs.
   You should have told me this was part of it."
They laughed and yelled and pushed me around.
Then some of them held me
   and one guy tried to open my mouth
   so he could pour the beer in,

and the guy with the needle moved in closer.
At first I had been mad.
Now I was afraid, Lord.
Somehow I was able to break loose from them.
     I ran for the side door.
They grabbed me by my jacket.
I pulled myself out of it
     and ran for home.
I was so scared, Lord!
I'm still scared.
I feel all shakey and sick inside.
And I'm worried.
How'll I face those kids at school tomorrow?
What shall I do?
And what'll I say to Dad when he asks me
     where my jacket is?
What do I do, Lord,
     what do I do?

Let's Talk

If you were in this boy's position, what would you do?

If this incident was reported to the principal of the school, what action might be taken?

Would the boy suffer in any way?

Have you ever had anyone try to force his or her beliefs on you?

How did you feel?

What did you say?

How did the others answer you?

Have Mom and Dad ever had anyone try to force his ideas on them?

How did they handle it?

It Helps to Remember

Compromising by lying to our parents or others is a trap that will harm us. When we refuse to do what we know is right, we put ourselves in a situation where we are an easy target for those who do wrong. We protect ourselves by obeying what we know to be right.

We have a right to make our own decisions and believe what we choose to believe. No one can take this right from us or force us to believe something we don't want to believe. We are wise if we avoid people who try to force or coax us into believing and doing what they do.

Verses to Remember

"If you continue in my word, you are truly my disciples, and you will know the truth, and the truth will make you free. . . . So if the Son makes you free, you will be free indeed" (John 8:31, 36).

26

A Ball Game or Dusting, Which Shall It Be?

Dear God,
    It's so neat the way Mom and Dad
    attend all my ball games.
Dad says,
    "I'll get up early tomorrow and go to the office and finish my
work,"
    and he closes his case.
"If you don't mind looking at the dust another day, I don't,"
    Mom says laughing.
    "Let's go!"
They bring chairs along,
    but they don't just sit there
    and yakkety-yak with their friends.
They watch every play
    and yell
    and cheer
    and honk the horn
    and jump up and down when I round home plate
    and call out, "Better luck next time!"
    when I strike out.
It's so neat, God, having them so excited about my ball playing.
Thank You, God.

Let's Talk

How do your mom and dad show interest in what you are doing?

Complete the sentence: "I wish my _____ was interested when I _____.

What are some of your dad's special interests? Try to guess first and then have him tell you.

Do the same for your mother.

How do you show interest in what your mom and dad are interested in?

Talk about how you can show interest in each other.

It Helps to Remember

One way we say "I love you" to our family and friends is to find out what interests them and then show our interest in their concerns.

A Verse to Remember

"Don't just think about your own affairs, but be interested in others, too, and in what they are doing" (Phil. 2:4, TLB).

27

Do I Play Soccer or Go to Church?

God, I have such a tough decision to make!
I want to play on the soccer team
    but they practice Sunday mornings.
I don't want to miss church and Sunday school,
    but I really want to play soccer.
What should I do?
I feel all mixed up inside.

Let's Talk

How do you feel when you have to make a decision and don't know what to do?

Tackling a problem helps us get rid of the feeling of frustration. Let's think about the problem. We'll call the girl who has the problem Sandy.

The decision Sandy has to make is whether to join the soccer team or go to church.

What are some of the alternatives Sandy has? Talk about this before you read the alternatives suggested below.

1. Sandy can choose to play soccer and forget about church.

2. Sandy can go to church and forget soccer.

3. Is it possible for Sandy to do both? Would the soccer team be willing to meet for practice at 11 a.m. or in the afternoon? Then Sandy could both go to church and play soccer.

4. Could Sandy go to church half the time and play soccer half the time?

5. Is there some other sport during the week in which Sandy could participate instead of soccer?

As Christians, when we make decisions, we bear three things in mind:

1. God wants us to love Him more than anything or anybody else. Has He said anything about Sunday?

2. God wants us to care about the happiness of others.

3. God wants us to care about ourselves.

Using these guidelines, if you were Sandy, what choice would you make?

If you chose No. 2, but it didn't work out, what would you choose next? Why?

How do you think you would feel about your decision? Why? Can Mom or Dad or the adults in your group share a decision they had to make and how they felt while they were making it and afterward?

Do you have a decision to make now? If so, talk about it.

It Helps to Remember

There are guidelines we can follow when making a decision:

1. State what decision must be made.

2. Write down all the different decisions we can make. What are our alternatives? Has God specifically said anything about it?

3. Think about what would happen in each case.

4. Choose the decision that we think is the best one.

5. If that doesn't work out, choose the next best alternative.

6. Do what we decided to do.

7. After doing it, evaluate our decision. How did it work out? How did we feel about it?

A Verse to Remember

"If any of you lacks wisdom, let him ask God, who gives to all men generously and without reproaching, and it will be given him" (James 1:5).

28

It's Not Just What You Say but How You Say It That Counts

It isn't just what Dad says, Lord;
    it's the way he says it
    that hurts sometimes.
The words say one thing,
    but his tone of voice says something else.
I wonder if Dad ever listens to his own voice;
    do You think so?

Let's Talk

What tone of voice don't you like? Can you mimic it?

How does that tone make you feel?

What tone of voice do you like? Mimic it.

How does that tone make you feel?

How about the adults in your group? What tones do they like or not like and why?

Can you think of someone who has a pleasant voice?

When we read the Bible, we don't know what the tone of the speaker was. For example, think of the different meanings this verse could have depending on the tone of voice:

"O Jerusalem, Jerusalem, killing the prophets and stoning those who are sent to you! How often would I have gathered your children together as a hen gathers her brood under her wings, and you would not!" (Matt. 23:37).

Read that verse as though Jesus was scolding.

Now read it as though Jesus was grieving.

What difference does it make?

When might it be all right to voice anger?

Practice saying the following words using different tones of voice:

You're the greatest.	All right.
Oh, yeah.	That's really nice.
No kidding.	I like it.
I wouldn't trust you.	I'm going to get you.
For sure.	Yes.
You look different.	No.
This food tastes different.	Forgive me.
I'm sorry.	

It Helps to Remember

The tone of our voice is as important as the words we say. Tones can encourage people and tell them we love them. Tones can hurt people and make them feel bad. Tones are affected by the way we feel in our hearts, so the best thing is to ask Jesus to give us good, clean, loving hearts. Tones are affected by what we think, so we need to ask Jesus to give us an understanding mind. And, even when we feel angry or frustrated, we can learn to control our voices and the tone of our voices.

A Verse to Remember

"Pleasant words are like a honeycomb,
  sweetness to the soul and health
  to the body" (Prov. 16:24).

29

I Didn't Promise to Baby-sit!

Lord, I'm upset again!
I was going to spend the night with Sheryl,
  but Mom promised Mrs. Spencer I'd baby-sit.
Why does she make promises like that
  without asking me first?

Let's Talk

Do your parents or other adults ever promise others that you will do something without asking you first?

How do you feel then?

Have Mom or Dad or the adults in your group ever had this happen to them?

How did they feel?

What is the best way to handle this problem?

It Helps to Remember

You have a right to be asked about decisions that affect you. If people make promises for you, you can say, "I will do it this time, but from now on, please talk to me first."

Remember to ask them kindly.

Verses to Remember

"You shall love your neighbor as yourself" (Mark 12:31).

"Love is . . . kind" (1 Cor. 13:4).

30

My Friend Doesn't Believe in Jesus

I have a new friend, Lord.
Ahamed is his name.
He's so different it's going to take some time
    to know how to be a good friend to him.
We became friends because I felt sorry for him
    and because he was kind to me.
All the other kids were pushing him around,
    calling him names
    and saying his people are oil gluttons
    and selfish and greedy and mean
    and charge much more for oil than they should.
I guess they talk that way because Ahamed's father came
    from Iran.
"Hey, lay off," I'd say,
    and Ahamed and I'd walk away together.
Ahamed sits right behind me in math class.
When I was having trouble solving a problem,
    he said, "Let me help you."
He was so good explaining things
    that in no time at all I understood and had the problem
    solved.
I said, "Thank you,"
    and he smiled his shy smile
    and we were friends.
We have fun playing chess together
    and riding our bikes
    and shooting baskets,
but I have to confess, Lord,
    that when we start to talk about You,

I get all mixed up.
Ahamed says he's a Muslim.
He knows all about Abraham and Isaac and the Old Testament,
    and he says he believes in You, Jesus,
        but not like I do.
He says You were a prophet, but only a prophet.
How could You be God, he asks, if a woman gave birth to You?
But he says he prays to God,
    and when he repeated some of his prayers,
        I thought, "Why, that's almost the way I pray."
He says he believes God is a God of mercy and love
    and that's what I believe,
    and he understands about sin and not lying and stealing,
    but instead we should be honest, kind and good,
    but no way will he say that You, Jesus, are God.
That mixes me all up, and I don't know what to do.
Dad says,
    "Just go on being his friend and loving him.
    When he is willing to accept it,
        you can let him read your New Testament.
    And maybe sometime later you can invite him
        to go to church with you.
But for now, just be his friend.
Talk to Mother.
Maybe you even can invite him to spend the night with you.
We'll pray for him
    and ask Jesus to help him understand."

Is just caring for my friend
    and letting him know I love him enough, Lord?
How can I get him to understand about You?

Let's Talk

Do you have any friends who are Mormons or Jews or Mus-
lims or Hindus?
    Have you ever talked with them about God?
    Do they respect you or make fun of you?
    Do you and your classmates at school respect them or do some

of the children sometimes make remarks that aren't kind?

What should our attitude be toward those who believe differently than we do?

Why is being a good friend important?

How can we be both good friends and good witnesses for Jesus?

How can you show your friend that you care about him or her as a person?

It Helps to Remember

We have a right to choose what to believe, but we also have a responsibility to respect the beliefs of others. Respect does not mean we have to agree with others' beliefs. It means we will not make fun of their beliefs.

We need to show them God's love by how we treat them.

A Verse to Remember

"Always be prepared to make a defense to any one who calls you to account for the hope that is in you, yet do it with gentleness and reverence" (1 Pet. 3:15).

31

Is My Room Really Mine?

Dear Lord,
Sometimes I'm not sure if my room
really is mine.
"It's your room," Mom says. "Fix it up like you want."
But if I don't keep my room as clean as Mom likes,
she gets on my case.
"If you don't clean your room,
we're going to move out the furniture," she says,
talking as though the room was her room,
and she could do anything with it that she wants.
That confuses me.
Whose room is it anyway?
If it's really my room,
does Mom have a right telling me
what to do with it?
But then, I wonder, maybe that's what parents are for—
to tell you what to do.
But I'm getting older, Lord.
I have some opinions of my own too.
Shouldn't parents be flexible too
and give their kids some rights and freedom?

Let's Talk

Do you have your own room at home?
What privileges go along with having your own room?
What responsibilities do you have in regard to having your own room?
Did your parents discuss this with you and together did you agree on this?

How do you feel when your room is messy?

How do you feel when your room is clean and in order?

Do you decorate your room as you wish or are there certain restrictions?

If there are certain restrictions, why do you suppose your parents have made them?

When you don't care for your room responsibly, how do Mom and Dad feel?

It Helps to Remember

Having our own room is a privilege not many children in the world have. In some countries families have no permanent homes, only makeshift shacks. In some cities a whole family will live in one room. So for a child to have a private room is special.

A private room gives us a place to get away and be alone. We should not confuse the idea, though, that a room of our own means it belongs to us. Our parents are paying for our use of the room and we need to respect their wishes. A private room may or may not mean the opportunity to decorate it the way we like. That needs to be discussed together, and we need to respect how our parents feel about it. Children have some rights, and parents have some rights. In a happy family children and parents think of each other.

A Verse to Remember

"Live in harmony with one another" (Rom. 12:16).

32

Lost!

Wow! was I scared today.
Daryl called me and asked me to come and play soccer with him.
I've never been to Daryl's house,
    but when he gave me the name of the street, I said,
        "Oh, I know where that is.
        It'll take me a little time though,
        because I'll have to ride over.
        Mom's not home."
I left a note for Mom,
    swung my leg over my bike and took off.
But when I came to 1916 Lodi,
    it wasn't Daryl's house.
"Maybe he lives at 1916 Lodi East," the lady said.
    "This is 1916 Lodi West."
I took off heading east,
    but after a few blocks the road dead-ended.
I circled around but couldn't find Lodi Street again.
    Instead, I realized I was lost—really lost.
I wondered what to do.
I wasn't sure I could even find my way home.
At last I came to a little store
    and outside was a pay phone.
Luckily I had a quarter
    and luckily Mom was home.
I explained what happened and then asked,
    "Can you tell me how to get to 1916 Lodi East, Mom?"
"Maybe," she said. "Where are you?"
"I don't know," I said. "I wouldn't have called you if I knew."
"Look around and find some street signs," she said.
I finally saw a street sign
    but there was a gang of really tough-looking kids

standing by it too,
    and they were eyeing me.
"There's some tough kids across the street," I said.
My heart was thumping,
    and I had to keep wetting my lips they were so dry.
"Go in the store," Mom said.
    "Tell the man where you want to go.
    If the street isn't close by,
        ask him how you can get back home.
    Wait till the kids go away.
    If they don't go away, call me.
    I'll come and get you."
I hung up and went inside the store.
You know how I was praying to You, Lord.
The man told me that 1916 Lodi East was just a block away.
I picked up a comic book and pretended I was reading
    while really I was watching those kids out of the corner
    of my eye.
After what seemed ten years they walked off.
I waited a little longer just to be sure they were really gone.
Then I rode my bike like crazy,
    following the store man's directions,
    found the street
    and Daryl standing outside his house waiting for me.
"Where've you been?" he asked. "To Alaska?"
"I made a mistake," I explained. "I should have asked you if you
    live east or west."
Next time I'll be sure I have *complete* directions, Lord.
I sure don't like getting lost.
It's scarey.

Let's Talk

Have you ever been lost?
How did you feel?
What did you do? Tell about it.
Have your mom and dad ever been lost? Ask them to tell
about their experience.

What information should we know that we can give to people when we are lost?

How can we know what people we can trust?

Talk about this with your parents.

It Helps to Remember

When we get lost, we sometimes get so scared we can't think clearly. It helps if we can learn to say to ourselves, "Calm down. Think about what is best to do." We need also to know our parents' full names, addresses and phone numbers and also the names, in full, of one or two neighbors.

Some cities have Block Parents. Block Parents put a little sign in their windows. It always is safe to run to the door of a house of a Block Parent if you are in trouble. They will help.

A Verse to Remember

"When I am afraid,
I put my trust in thee" (Ps. 56:3).

33

Michael's My Best Friend

Dear God,
It was so good today to see Michael again.
"Did you have a fun Christmas at your uncle's?" I asked.
"No," he said, "I'd rather have been with you."
We sat quiet-like, not talking,
    and ate all the cookies Mom had given us.
Michael knocked over his orange juice accidentally,
    but I cleaned it up for him.
And then we played Atari baseball.
I think he let me win.
We watched a TV show,
    and it was so funny we laughed and laughed.
Mom said Michael could stay for dinner
    if it was all right with his mom.
We called, and she said, "Sure."
Dad drove Michael home at nine,
    and I went along.
Today has been such a happy day.
Thank You, God, and thank You for a friend like Michael.
A best friend just has to be one of the best things we can have.

Let's Talk

    Who is your best friend?
    What do you enjoy doing together?
    What do you like most about your friend?
    Who is your dad's best friend?
    Your mom's?
    What do they like most about their friends?
    What do they enjoy doing with their friends?

In 1 Samuel 18:1-4 we read about two young men who became good friends. How did Jonathan show David he loved him?

How can we be Jesus' friend? (John 15:14).

It Helps to Remember

Everybody needs one or two friends to whom he can tell almost everything and who understands him. Friends are so important we need to choose them wisely and then take time to be with each other.

A Verse to Remember

"A friend loves at all times" (Prov. 17:17).

34

I Like Going to Michael's House

Thank You, Lord, for Michael
   who is such an understanding friend.
When Michael asks me to spend the night with him,
   we have so much fun!
His mom makes pizza
   and we have popcorn later
   and when we go to bed,
      Michael puts his big dog, Nugget,
      outside for the night
      even though Nugget usually sleeps inside.
Michael knows I'm not used to dogs
   and can't sleep well because I'm always wondering
   when Nugget will start to lick my face,
   and I don't like it when he lies on me.
At breakfast Michael's mom doesn't make me eat a lot
   because she understands
   I'm not hungry till later.
And when Michael and I go out to play,
   we skate
   because Michael knows how much I love it.
Thank You, God, for Michael,
   who knows what I like
   and tries to make me happy.
When he comes to my house, I'll do the same for him.

Let's Talk

Are there certain things you don't like to eat?

If your friend invites you and has food for lunch that you don't like, how do you feel?

Are there certain things you don't like to do?

How do you feel when your friend insists you do them?

How do you feel when your friend suggests you do things that you really enjoy doing?

It Helps to Remember

We make and keep friends when we learn what they like and don't like. Then when they visit us, we do all we can to make them comfortable and happy. We try to serve them food they like, and we try to do things they enjoy doing.

We also make and keep friends by willingly doing what the other wants—despite how we may feel at times. We don't complain or insist on our own way.

A Verse to Remember

"Let each of you look not only to his own interests, but also to the interests of others" (Phil. 2:4).

35

What's in a Name?

Today I became a person in math class.
My teacher finally called me by name.
"Rob, what answer did you get?" she asked.
Up until now she has looked at me when I have raised my hand.
"Yes?" she has said.
"Yes" isn't my name.
Rob is,
  but she hasn't known me by name until today.
I felt so good!
No longer am I just one of her students.
I'm Rob,
  and I like being Rob,
  and I like hearing my name.

Let's Talk

How do you feel when someone calls you by name?
What is your middle name?
What are the middle names of those in your family?
Do you like your names?
If you could have chosen your name, what name would you have chosen? Talk about this.
What do your names mean?
Do you have any nicknames?
Do you like your nicknames?
What do you want your parents to call you?
What do you want your brothers or sisters to call you?
What do you want your friends to call you?

Do you know what your friends want you to call them? Ask them.

How do you address the friends of your parents?

Do you call them by their first names or do you say "Mr." and "Mrs."? Which do you think they prefer?

How do you feel when someone mispronounces your name?

It Helps to Remember

People are sensitive about their names. It is important to know both the first and last name of our friends so we can introduce them to others. People also like to be called by certain names. Sometimes they dislike nicknames that have been given them. If that is so, it is courteous not to call them by those names. People also like to have their names pronounced correctly.

Some people have a hard time remembering names and others meet and work with so many people it is difficult for them to remember everyone's name. If someone forgets our name, we should remember that there may be a good reason for it. We should not be too sensitive about it.

A Verse to Remember

"I have called you by name, you are mine" (Isa. 43:1).

36

Relatives

What a neat surprise to get to know our Uncle Jim, Lord!
He'd been only a name before.
When Mom said he was coming for a visit,
    I groaned and thought,
        "There goes my bed!"
I didn't know how much fun he would be.
He wanted to see my school
    and our classroom
    and he looked through my books
    and then he asked if he could go along
        with us after school to the park.
We stopped on the way for a triple-scoop ice-cream cone.
At the park he said if it'd be okay, he'd be umpire.
He was a whiz.
After dinner I got stuck on a math problem,
       and he helped me.
I didn't wake up when he crawled in bed later;
    he was so quiet.
When he left this morning,
    he gave me an envelope.
Inside was a note
    and an air ticket to come to see him!
"You must see our home and church and where I work," he
wrote.
    "How about going along with me to play golf?
    And do you like to swim?
    You can help me on my day off
        when I deliver Meals on Wheels.
We need to get to know each other,
    because we really are family."
Goodness, Lord, I never knew before

how nice it is to have relatives.
What a surprise!
Uncle Jim can have my bed any time.

Let's Talk

How many of your relatives can you name?

Do you know what work your uncles and aunts do?

Outside of your own family, who are your favorite relatives? Why?

Do you have some relatives you don't know well?

If so, can Mom and Dad tell you something about them?

If you don't know your relatives very well, how do you feel when they come to visit you or you go to visit them?

What can you do to get to know your relatives better?

It Helps to Remember

Grandparents, uncles, aunts and cousins can be super friends for us. Because we belong to the same family, they are often naturally interested in us. Sometimes it's very easy to talk to them —at times it is easier to talk with them than to talk to our parents. Sometimes they may even have more time for us than our parents do. Some parents are very busy, while grandparents are often retired. Taking time to get to know our relatives is worthwhile.

A Verse to Remember

"A brother is born to help in time of need" (Prov. 17:17, TLB).

37

My Sister Always Cuts Me Down

I'm miserable, Lord.
My sister is always cutting me down.
She keeps telling me how stupid I am to spend so much time
    studying.
I *like* to study.
She thinks the way I wear my hair is weird
    and that I wear the dumbest clothes.
She says I'm always saying the wrong things
    and that I'll never have any boyfriends.
She's driving me crazy—how long will I have to listen to her?
If we didn't have to share a room,
    I could get away from her.
I hate myself, Lord!
I hate my sister!
Why do I have to be me,
    and why do I have to be part of this family?

Let's Talk

Do you know someone who is always cutting you down?
How does it make you feel?
What things do your parents say that make you feel good about yourself?
What things do your parents say that make you feel small and no-good?
Now ask your parents if they have trouble with this. Do they know people who make them feel like they're not worth very much?

What do people do or say to make them feel this way?

How do they handle their feelings when this happens?

Sometimes do you say things about your parents that make them feel small or foolish? Ask them.

When people constantly cut us down, could they be having personal problems that make them attack us? What might be some of the things bothering them?

Does realizing this change your attitude?

What can we do for them?

It Helps to Remember

If someone "cuts us down," we need to first remember who we are. God has made us and loves us without any conditions. We are never worthwhile because we are conforming to others' standards. We are worthwhile because God loves and accepts us the way we are. What people say can never change that.

People who constantly "cut down" others usually have personal problems. They may not feel loved or worthwhile and so they are jealous. Loving them and showing them that we love them is the best way to respond to them. Talk about practical ways to do this.

Remember, too, we can help people to become better persons by encouraging them and emphasizing their good points instead of calling attention to their weaknesses.

Verses to Remember

"Whenever we can we should always be kind to everyone, and especially to our Christian brothers" (Gal. 6:10, TLB).

"Love your enemies, do good to those who hate you, bless those who curse you, pray for those who abuse you" (Luke 6:27, 28).

38

Why Didn't Mother Come?

Dear Lord,
I feel so, so sad.
It was awful a year ago
    when Mom and Dad said they were going to get a divorce.
I couldn't believe it!
I didn't say much,
    but I felt like I had gone all to pieces inside.
I was happy, though, when they decided
    that Tony and I would live with Dad.
Mom said she would come on weekends
    and take Tony and me home with her by turns.
That's what's been tough.
She's always on time when it's Tony's weekend,
    and she makes a big fuss over him.
But when it's my weekend,
    she's always late,
    and I mean late,
        really late.
I sit on the doorstep and wait and wait,
    and when she finally comes,
    she gives me a little peck on the cheek
    and sighs and says,
        "Let's go. I've got lots to do."
Today, Lord,
    I sat on the steps
    and waited and waited
    and waited and waited.
She *never* came.
Right now I don't want to see her again, Lord.
Never, Never, NEVER!

Let's Talk

Why do you think the mother never came?

Why does she treat the boy differently?

If this happened to a friend of yours, what would you say or do to help?

When the boy finally sees his mother, what should he do or say?

It Helps to Remember

There may be many reasons why a parent seems to like one child more than another. Sometimes a child may look like his father, and the divorced mother doesn't want to be reminded of her former husband. Sometimes certain personality differences make it hard for people to get along. The boy needs help in finding out just why his mother treats him as she does. If friends can't help, sometimes a pastor or a family counselor can. He should ask for help.

If your parents are divorced or are struggling in the home, remember that their lives are being torn to pieces. They are hurt and probably very unhappy with themselves. This means they may react in impatience toward everyone in the family, including you. Remember they are hurting, too. Hurt people often do things that hurt others.

Verses to Remember

"Turn thou to me, and be gracious to me;
   for I am lonely and afflicted.
Relieve the troubles of my heart,
   and bring me out of my distresses" (Ps. 25:16, 17).
"For my father and my mother have forsaken me, but the
   Lord will take me up" (Ps. 27:10).
"I will not fail you or forsake you. Be strong and of good cour-
   age" (Josh. 1:5, 6).

39

Why Did Uncle Tim Divorce Aunt Ruth?

I spent all morning in the nurse's office at school, Lord.
My stomach hurt something terrible.
At breakfast, when she was talking to Dad,
    Mom spilled it that Uncle Tim is divorcing Aunt Ruth.
I couldn't believe it.
Not my favorite Uncle Tim!
What'll happen to Stephanie and Joel?
Who'll they live with?
Where'll Uncle Tim live?
What will Aunt Ruth do?
Lord, I can't understand it,
    but my stomach sure hurts.

Let's Talk

Have any of your relatives or friends divorced?
How did you feel when you got the news?
Why did you feel that way?
What helped you feel better?
Do you know of some children in divorced homes who are happy?
Why did Uncle Tim divorce Aunt Ruth?

It Helps to Remember

Living a life of obedience to God will protect us from many of the problems people face in life.

Certain hard experiences come to everyone, but with Jesus as our helper we shall be able to live through them. Jesus invites us to tell Him about everything that troubles us. We can trust Him to work things out for our highest good.

A Verse to Remember

"Let him have all your worries and cares, for he is always thinking about you and watching everything that concerns you" (1 Pet. 5:7, TLB).

40

But I Don't Want to Play Ball!

Dad signed me up for Little League, Lord,
  but I don't want to play ball.
I want to be on the chess team.
He came home with this new bat and glove
  and was all excited.
He swung the bat and said,
  "I've been waiting and waiting for you
    to be old enough to play on the team.
  I'll practice with you every night,
    and we'll make you into the home-run champion of the
    year."
He swung his bat again.
"Now when I was your age," he began.
I sighed and turned off my ears from the inside.
When he finally stopped,
  I took a deep breath
  and all in a rush said,
    "I don't want to play ball."
"You don't what?" he asked.
"I want to play chess," I said.
My voice was very small,
  and I felt small too.
"You what?" he exploded.
He stared at me and then
  walked out
  and slammed the door so hard the dog howled.
I crawled off to bed.
Mom came up to my room later.
"No dinner?" she asked.
"No," I said. "I feel sick."

"Flu?" Mom asked.

"Maybe."

How do I tell her what the real trouble is, Lord?

And what do I do

   so Dad won't be mad at me anymore?

And do I have to play ball?

Let's Talk

Have adults ever insisted that you do something you really didn't like or want to do?

How did you feel?

What did you do?

Have your mom or dad or the adults in your group ever had this happen to them? How did they feel? What did they do?

Sometimes it may happen that our parents or teachers suggest we do something, and to begin with we say, "No." The reason we don't want to do it may be that we think we won't be able to do it well. But then we try and find out we can do it, and we begin to like it. Have you ever had an experience like that?

It Helps to Remember

We should communicate with our parents about the way we want to spend our leisure time. We need to help them understand us as individuals. It may help them to respect our wishes.

Sometimes we hesitate about our parents' choices for us because we're afraid we can't do something well. Our parents may see that we need to be challenged to grow up in that area of our lives. Then we have to risk failure and try. Often we succeed.

A Verse to Remember

"Give your burdens to the Lord, He will carry them" (Ps. 55:22, TLB).

41

What Do You Mean, "I'm Better Than You"?

My sister, Mary, tells me she is better than me, Lord.
I wonder if that is really true.
I'm not as pretty as my sister,
    but I can run faster.
She is smarter than me at math,
    but I do better than her in English.
She has more friends than I,
    but Mother calls me her good helper.
Sometimes I feel jealous of Mary
    because she is pretty
    and good at math
    and has lots of friends.
When those feelings come, Jesus,
    help me to ask You to chase them out of my mind right away.
    Help me not to spend time thinking worthless thoughts.
    Help me instead to start thanking You for all I can do well.
Thank You for making me as I am.
Help me to become better in the things I can do.
Most of all, Jesus,
    help all of us
    become more like You.
And thank You that You loved us,
    just as we are,
    enough to die for us.

Let's Talk

What does your sister or brother do better than you?

How does this make you feel?

What do you say when you feel this way?

What things do you do better than your sister or brother?

How do you think this makes them feel?

What do they say?

Did the adults in your group ever feel they weren't as good as their sisters or brothers or classmates? Ask them to tell you about it.

Do they still sometimes feel they aren't as good as the people they live and work with?

How do these feelings affect them?

Because there are some things you do not do as well as your brothers or sisters or friends, does this mean they are better persons than you?

If someone boasts that he can do something better than you, how can you answer that person?

It Helps to Remember

There are many things I cannot do as well as other people, but that doesn't mean I am not a worthwhile person. Sometimes I wonder if there is anything I can do well—at least when I look at others. Yet, God never asked me to compare myself with others. God gave me the abilities I have. He loves me as I am, and He will help me every day to become the person He wants me to be. What I am as a person is more important than what I can do. His approval of me makes my life worthwhile, not what I can do better than others.

A Verse to Remember

". . . you are precious in my eyes, and honored, and I love you" (Isa. 43:4).

42

Does Dad Love Rachel More Than Me?

Sometimes, Lord, I worry that Dad likes my sister more than me.
When I tell him about something that has happened in school,
    Dad stays hidden behind his paper,
    or his eyes stay on the TV screen,
    and he just sorta' grunts, "Uh, huh."
But when Rachel talks,
    well, now, that's different!
Dad throws down his paper
    and pulls Rachel up on his knee
    and his eyes sparkle
    and he laughs and laughs
    or rubs her back if the news is sad.
What makes the difference, Lord?
Why doesn't Dad show me as much love as he does Rachel?
When I see him enjoying Rachel so much,
    I get real quiet
    and go off to my room
    and sit on my bed.
Sometimes Rachel comes in and tries to be loving.
I think she knows I'm hurting.
I push her away—I can't help it—
    and bury my head in the pillow
    so she won't see my tears.
Sometimes she'll wait a little,
    and then she says,
    "I'm sorry,"
    and rubs my back,
    and it helps

even if I find it hard to tell her
    that it helps.
But I wish I wouldn't have to worry and wonder
    if Dad really doesn't love me as much
    as he loves Rachel.
I wish he would treat both of us the same.

Let's Talk

Do you ever feel that your mom or dad or your teachers love someone else more than they love you?

How does this make you feel?

How do you react?

Do your mother or father or teachers sometimes say things or do things that make you feel you are not as good as your brother or sister? Give examples.

Have the adults in your family ever been jealous of a brother or sister of theirs because they thought their parents loved the other child more?

What happened that made them feel this way?

How did they act when they felt this way?

How did they get rid of their jealousy or do they still feel jealous?

Do parents love all their children in exactly the same way? Explain.

Do children love their dad in the same way they love their mother? Explain.

It Helps to Remember

We get jealous when we think our parents love a brother or sister more than us. We need to understand that because children are different from each other, parents will love each child in a different way. The love expressed may appear different but is of the same quality.

Some parents may not be sensitive to their children's needs. Problems in the lives of our parents may affect their love for us or the way they express it. If there seems to be a lack of love or concern for you by your parents, remember that you are not the cause. Parents often struggle with difficult problems, and it may affect their love for us.

Verses to Remember

"Now there are varieties of gifts, but the same Spirit. . . . If the foot should say, 'Because I am not a hand, I do not belong to the body,' that would not make it any less a part of the body" (1 Cor. 12:4, 15). Ask your parents to explain this verse.

"See to it . . . that no 'root of bitterness' spring up and cause trouble, and by it the many become defiled" (Heb. 12:15).

43

Curiosity Usually Doesn't Kill Cats or Kids

"Questions, questions, questions,
   you're always asking questions!" Dad says,
   and today he sounds irritated.
Don't grown-ups have questions, Lord?
If they do, why do they sometimes answer us kids the way they
do when we ask questions?—
   "I don't have time to answer your question."
   "You wouldn't understand the answer."
   "It's too complicated to explain."
   "I don't know."
   "You don't need to know why. Just do what I tell you."
   "That's a dumb question."
Why do grown-ups give answers like these, Lord?
Don't they know when children have questions
   they either feel really excited and want to find answers,
   or they feel a little nervous,
   or puzzled,
   or afraid?
Why don't grown-ups stop and think how we feel
   when we ask questions?
Sometimes they don't take time
   to really answer our questions.

Let's Talk

Have you ever been told not to ask so many questions?
Questions about what?

How did it make you feel?

How do you feel when you ask questions and adults only say, "Uh, huh" and don't answer your questions?

What could you say, politely and kindly, to get an answer to your question when adults give the excuses listed below? Discuss each statement.

1. "I don't have time to answer your question."
2. "You wouldn't understand the answer."
3. "It's too complicated to explain."
4. "I don't know the answer."
5. "You don't need to know why. Just do what I tell you."
6. "That's a dumb question."

Have your mom or dad or adults in your group ever been told not to ask questions? Ask them to tell about it. How did they feel?

Are there certain situations and circumstances when it is not right, proper or courteous for us to ask questions? Discuss.

It Helps to Remember

Curiosity can lead to learning. If we ask because we want to learn more or grow in understanding, and we are not prying into private affairs, it is good to ask questions.

Sometimes we need to recognize that we may be asking questions at the wrong time. Maybe our parents are busy or thinking about something else. Maybe we should learn to ask at a better time.

Verses to Remember

"Ask, and it will be given you; seek, and you will find; knock, and it will be opened to you. For every one who asks receives, and he who seeks finds, and to him who knocks it will be opened" (Matt. 7:7, 8).

44

Do Adults Really Expect Me to Lie?

I can't understand it, Lord.
Grown-ups teach us in Sunday school and church to be honest,
　　but in everyday life
　　grown-ups sometimes expect us not to tell the truth.
For example, today I got mad and hit Michael.
"Say you're sorry!" Dad thundered,
　　holding my arm tightly.
Maybe I didn't do right hitting Mike,
　　but I really wasn't sorry.
He had been teasing me about my red hair,
　　and I was mad.
And then there was the time my Aunt Mary sent me the silliest
　　T-shirt with "Piece-of-cake" printed on it.
Just because I say "piece-of-cake" a lot,
　　does she think I want a shirt
　　with that printed on it?
Mom thought it was cute.
"Tell Aunt Mary how much you like the shirt," she says,
　　standing over me to get me to write a thank-you note.
Is she kidding, Lord?
Does she really want me to write that?
I hate the shirt!
I'll never wear it.
Or how about it, Lord, when the phone rings
　　and Mom says,
　　　　"If it's Mrs. Jones again,
　　　　I'm not home!"
I can't say that!

Mom's right there beside me!
I can't understand, Lord, why adults expect kids to lie.
Do they lie?

Let's Talk

Have you sometimes told lies?

Have you sometimes been asked to tell lies?

Have Mom or Dad or the adults in your group been asked to say something that isn't true? Talk about this.

Instead of saying, "I'm sorry I hit you, Michael," what answer could have been given that would have been both appropriate and honest?

Instead of writing to Aunt Mary: "I really liked the shirt you sent me," what could have been written that would have been both honest and kind?

When somebody calls and the adult doesn't want to answer, what message can be given that is both honest and courteous?

How do we feel when we can respond in a way that is both honest and courteous?

It Helps to Remember

God has told us always to be honest. If we feel that someone is asking us to not be truthful, we can ask them to respect our desires and to not ask us to lie. It might be that we have misunderstood them.

A Verse to Remember

"Do not lie to one another" (Col. 3:9).

45

I Just Want to Be Me!

Sometimes it's hard being a kid, Lord.
Everyone expects so much of you.
Mom wants me to take piano and ballet lessons.
I want to play ball.
Aaron, my brother, wants me to wait on him,
    but I can't see why he can't wait on me, too, sometimes.
Grandma wants me to wear dresses.
I like jeans.
My friend Lee wants me to do everything she wants to do,
    but I have some ideas of my own.
My teacher wants me to try out for our class play,
    but I'd rather be a cheerleader.
My dad wants me to earn a Ph.D.,
    whatever that is,
    but I'd rather do things with my hands
    than use my head and study books.
Everybody has an idea about what I should be.
I want to be just me.
But I feel bad sometimes, God,
    because I feel I'm not good enough
    to please *anybody*
    when I don't try to do
    what others want me to do.
But when I try to be what others want me to be,
    I feel all unhappy inside.
Is it wrong for me to want to be just me?

Let's Talk

What do you think: is it wrong for each of us to want to be just ourselves?

Do others wish you were different than you are?

How do you know? What do they expect of you?

How does this make you feel?

Have your mom or dad or the adults in your group had this experience?

How have others wished your mom and dad were different from what they are?

How has this made them feel?

Did they try to please others?

What is the difference between our having the right to be "just me" and our perhaps having to change some of the things we do?

It Helps to Remember

How we feel, how we respond to people, how we think, how we show or don't show our feelings, what interests us, what our habits are, what our disposition is like (sunny or moody, slow or quick), all of these add up to make each of us a distinct and different person. We say we are unique. That is, there is no one in the whole wide world exactly like us. God created each of us different. It is all right for us to be different. It is all right for me to be "just me."

However, because I live with other people and because God wants me to think about making them happy too, I may need to change some of the ways I do things. Who knows, maybe I'll enjoy what they want me to try! Talk about this.

Verses to Remember

When Jesus chose His disciples, they all were different from each other. Jesus recognized they were different and didn't insist they all had to be alike. For example, He said to Peter, "You are Peter." That is, "You are Peter. You aren't John or Andrew or Thomas or Matthew. You are Peter. And I accept you as you are, and I will have a work for you to do, Peter, that only you can do because you are Peter."

At the same time the Apostle Paul wrote in Philippians 2:4: "Let each of you look not only to his own interests, but also to the interests of others."

So we can be just ourselves, but at the same time we need to remember always to be considerate of others. Doing what they want us to do does not change who I am or the things I value.

46

Grandma Helped Me Feel Forgiven

I felt so bad, Lord.
We were at Grandma's house
    and she had this doll she used to play with
    lying in the little crib her dad had made for her.
Tim and I were wrestling just for fun,
    and I fell on the crib
    and the doll flew out
    and its head cracked in a thousand pieces.
Grandma's face looked so sad when she saw it.
I started to pick up the pieces
    and waited to hear her say,
      "How many times have I told you two boys
        to do your wrestling outside?"
But she didn't say anything.
She just got down on her knees
    and helped me pick up the pieces.
I felt so awful.
I started to cry.
"There, there," Grandma said, patting my shoulder,
    "I should have kept it in our bedroom
      if I didn't want to risk getting it broken.
    Any of us could have stumbled over it
      here in the family room."
"But you've told us not to wrestle in the house,"
    I sniffed. "I'm sorry."
"I know you are," Grandma said. "I'm sure you won't again.
    And we won't feel too bad about the doll.
    Sure I liked it.
    It's been fun having it all these years

and remembering when I was young like you.
But Grandpa and I are moving to a smaller house soon,
    and then we'll have to give away some of our things.
I don't know what I would have done with the doll,
    but I've been wanting to give you my softball."
"Your softball?" I asked.
    "*You* played softball, Grandma?
    I thought you only played dolls."
Grandma laughed,
    and when she laughs,
    it's like our wind chimes tinkling.
"You forget I had three brothers," she said, kissing me.
    "Now here's the ball.
    Outside you go.
    I'll call you when it's time for lunch."

Can you beat it, Lord, that's all she said.
She didn't get mad or even scold me.
Instead, she made me feel so good and forgiven, Lord.
And loved.
I'll bet not many kids have a grandma like mine.
Thank You so much for her!

Let's Talk

When you have broken something that has belonged to someone, has anything he said or did helped you feel better?
    Has anybody broken anything of yours?
    What did you say or do?
    Can Mom or Dad or the adults in your group share an inci-
dent when this happened to them?

It Helps to Remember

Forgiving people and making them feel more comfortable
after they have wronged us in some way is important. It expresses
love like Jesus had. It also leads to a happy family and close
friends.

A Verse to Remember

"He who forgives an offense seeks love,
but he who repeats a matter
alienates a friend" (Prov. 17:9).

47

So What If I'm Late?

Wow! Mom and Dad really did it.
But I guess I had it coming.
I'm usually late when we're going to leave for church.
"It upsets me," Mom says.
"I hate being late," Dad storms.
Finally he said,
    "Next time you're not ready
    on time,
    we're going to leave you."
I didn't really think they would,
    but they did!
Here I sit all alone in this big house, Lord.
I wonder what Mom and Dad will say
    when my friends ask where I am.
What a bummer!
I guess it was my fault,
    but what's so bad about being a little late?
I feel both guilty and mad, Lord.

Let's Talk

Is anybody in your family always late?
How does this make the others feel?
What have you as a family done to try to correct this?
Have you been successful?
Why is being late rude and inconsiderate?

It Helps to Remember

Being on time shows our respect for other people's time and commitments. It is unkind to always make others wait. Being late may accidentally happen, but it should never become a habit.

A Verse to Remember

"Live in harmony with one another" (Rom. 12:16).

48

I Don't Want My Sister to Wear My Sweater

Why do I have to have a sister, Lord?
Melanie's always wearing my sweaters.
I don't like the way they smell
    after she wears them.
"Wear your own!" I say.
"Yours are prettier," she says.
    "Besides, I don't have a pink or brown one."
Do I have to put up with this, Lord?
What can I do?

Let's Talk

Does your brother or sister or friend sometimes use something of yours without permission?

How do you feel?

How do you solve this problem?

Does nagging help?

How do you feel when someone nags or scolds because you've done something to irritate them?

Do you argue?

How do you feel after you've had a big argument?

Do Mom and Dad or the adults in your group ever have people borrow from them without getting permission?

What do they do to handle this situation?

It Helps to Remember

Trying to solve problems without nagging or arguments prevents bad feelings. If someone borrows something of yours without permission, keep your voice quiet and controlled. Tell the other person how you feel when they do this. Ask if there isn't some way the two of you can solve the problem. Tell them you want to keep a good relationship with them and to not end up with bad feelings toward them.

Verses to Remember

"Let us then pursue what makes for peace" (Rom. 14:19).
"Be at peace with one another" (Mark 9:50).

49

When Things Get Broken

I'm all mixed up inside tonight, Lord.
Mom has this Sunday school class
    with little kids whose parents are poor
    and never go to church.
Those kids are wild, Lord,
    I mean really wild.
Mom had a party for them here today at our house.
Everything was okay until it was time for refreshments.
I went into the kitchen to help Mom,
    and some of the kids tore off upstairs.
So we called them down.
They chased around like crazy down here,
    but we finally got them settled down,
    fed,
    and in the car to take them home.
But afterward, Lord—it still makes me angry when I think of it—
    I went upstairs
    and found the legs of my Barbie doll broken
    and the head off one of them,
    and they had broken Mike's bank open
    and the money was gone.
I was so angry with those kids.
But then I thought of what one little boy said
    as he got out of our car:
        "I wish I had a lucky home like yours with
        both a mommie and daddy."
I feel so bad when I think of that, Lord.
My feelings are all mixed up.
I'm both mad and sad.
"I guess," I said to Mom,
    as we were cleaning up the mess together,

"I guess next time we have a party for them,
we'll have to have it outdoors in a park
where there's nothing to tempt them
and where they can't break anything."

Let's Talk

Do you have any rough children in your school or church who break things?

Have they broken any of your things?

How did you feel?

Have you ever broken anything that belonged to someone else?

How did you feel?

What did you do?

It Helps to Remember

As we try to be friends with those who have not had the opportunities we have, we may see some of our property damaged. We have to be patient, forgiving and wise as we try to teach them to respect the property of others. And if someone breaks something of ours and even if he or she isn't sorry, still we should forgive them. Becoming angry and staying angry does us more harm than having our things broken.

We need to remember also that if we have broken something that belongs to someone else, we first should tell him or her how sorry we are. We also should offer to replace or pay for what we have broken.

Verses to Remember

"See that none of you repays evil for evil, but always seek to do good to one another and to all" (1 Thess. 5:15)

"Owe no one anything" (Rom. 13:8).

"Let us not grow weary in well-doing" (Gal. 6:9).

50

Having Someone Cheer for You Helps

I can hardly believe it, Lord.
I won the race.
I actually did!
I don't think I could have
    if Adam hadn't kept screaming,
        "You can do it, Mark.
        Run! Run! Run!
        Pour it on!"
It's great to have a friend who believes in you.
Thank you, Lord, for Adam.

Let's Talk

Do you have a friend who believes in you and encourages you?
How do you feel when you are with this friend?
Think of some time when Mom or Dad encouraged you.
Can Mom or Dad or the adults in your group think of some time when you encouraged them?
Who encourages your mom and dad most? How?
How do they feel when someone encourages them?
Take a few minutes and write down the things you think you would like to do and think you could do well if you tried hard.
Ask Mom and Dad to do the same.
Read your lists and discuss them. Do others in your family think there are things you could do well that you haven't put on your lists?
Decide to cheer for each other.

It Helps to Remember

When someone encourages us, we feel motivated to try even harder to succeed. When someone cheers for us and tells us he or she is sure we can do whatever we are trying to do, we get all charged up and find we *can* do more than we had thought we could do.

A Verse to Remember

The Apostle Paul wrote about Tychicus that Paul was sending him to the Christians at Ephesus, "that he may encourage your hearts" (Eph. 6:22).

51

Some Days I Need to Get Away from It All

Thank You, Lord, for a mother who understands.
You know how everything has been going wrong for me.
Monday night I fell asleep baby-sitting,
    and Mrs. Jones was super mad.
Wednesday the math test was really hard,
    and my mark was low.
Thursday I lost out when we had try-outs for our class play.
Jenny was supposed to stay overnight with me last night,
    but instead she went to Janet's house.
All week long everything has gone wrong.
I woke up this morning feeling so sad,
    wishing I could go horseback riding on the beach
    and forget it all.
But Saturdays usually I help Mom.
Mom knew something was wrong.
"What would you really like to do?" she asked,
    as I took out the vacuum cleaner.
    "Sometimes we all need a change."
"I'd like to go horseback riding," I said,
    "but it wouldn't be fair to leave all the work with you."
"Why not?" she asked. "You can do extra for me sometime
    when I'm feeling low.
    I think you should go.
    Get your brother to go with you."
"Really?" I asked.
"Really," she said, giving me a hug
    and a ten-dollar bill.
Getting away helped.
Jim and I galloped along the beach.

The wind whipped our faces.
My hair streamed out behind me.
I loved the salty taste when I licked my lips.
We rode faster and faster.
After a while we tethered our horses
    and lay in a sheltered cove.
We listened to the breakers crashing in on the shore
    and watched the gulls circling overhead
    and the little crabs scuttling into their holes.
We ate the lunch mother had sent along.
It tasted so good!
On the way home we passed a boy standing by the side of the
    road selling flowers.
I bought pink roses for Mom.
"They match your cheeks," she said when I gave them to her,
    and she kissed me.

Let's Talk

How do you think the girl felt when her mother suggested she go horseback riding?

How do you think the mother felt when she got the roses?

How do you feel when someone is sensitive to how you are feeling and makes allowances for it? Can you think of any examples?

When do you think parents should make allowances for their children?

When do you think children should make allowances for parents?

Can Mom and Dad share examples when someone has showed them they appreciate them? How has it made them feel?

It Helps to Remember

Being sensitive to how people feel is one way of saying, "I love you." Finding ways of meeting people's needs is another way of saying, "I love you." Expressing appreciation when somebody understands or helps us in something all of us can do. It helps us keep the friends we have. It makes people feel rewarded and it motivates them to continue helping and giving.

A Verse to Remember

"Give, and it will be given to you; good measure, pressed down, shaken together, running over, will be put into your lap. For the measure you give will be the measure you get back" (Luke 6:38).

52

I Hate It When Teachers Yell

Sometimes it's tough to be a kid, Lord.
Adults seem to have all the advantages.
Take teachers.
Teachers are adults.
They have the advantages.
We can't bad-mouth them,
    but they can yell at us as much as they want.
It isn't fair!
I start to sizzle and burn inside
    or else I just feel really down.
Sometimes I wish I could grow up really fast
    and be the principal,
    and I'd get even!
But I know that isn't right.
So I try to remember they are persons too
    and ask myself what I can learn from it all.

Let's Talk

Why do you think teachers yell? Think of all the reasons you can.

What do you do when they yell?

Do you ever deserve it?

Have Mom or Dad ever had people at work who have yelled at them or made life miserable for them?

How have they handled this?

When you've had a difficult day at school or work, do you

sometimes come home and "take it out" on your mom or dad or sisters or brothers?

How can we avoid this?

Take a few minutes and pray for those who make life difficult for us.

It Helps to Remember

Many people haven't learned to handle their frustrations in any other way than by yelling or fighting. When people yell at us for no reason, we need to learn not to mind their yelling. We can say to ourselves, "He or she is having a problem, but the problem isn't me. It's something else." Praying helps too.

If we truly did wrong and brought the problem on ourselves, we need to be quick to apologize.

Verses to Remember

"See that none of you repays evil for evil, but always seek to do good to one another and to all. Rejoice always, pray constantly, give thanks in all circumstances; for this is the will of God in Christ Jesus for you" (1 Thess. 5:15-18).

53

Making Your Friend Feel Special

Nancy is so special, Lord.
I'm so glad she's my friend.
I don't know how she can play the piano so well
    when she can't see.
I love to listen to her play.
"That's beautiful, Nancy," I say.
"Did you like it?" she says smiling.
"Nancy, you're always smiling," I say.
"Why not?" she says. "I'm happy."
And then she just smiles some more
    and squeezes my hand.
She's so special, God.
Thank You for a friend like Nancy.

Let's Talk

What makes some of your friends special?
What do your friends say is special about you?
What is special about each one in your family? Talk about
this.

It Helps to Remember

Everybody is special in one or many ways. Have you learned
to appreciate the "specialness" of people and tell them you
appreciate them? You may feel embarrassed about it, but do it
anyway. You'll feel great afterward!

Verses to Remember

"I thank my God in all my remembrance of you, always in every prayer of mine for you all making my prayer with joy" (Phil. 1:3, 4).

54

Why Are Clothes So Important?

I wish clothes weren't such a big deal, Lord.
Why do they make such a difference?
If I don't wear the latest thing—
    no matter how weird it looks—
or if I don't wear designer jeans
or name-brand clothes,
    the kids say,
        "What a loner!"
    or, "Why can't you get pants like ours?"
    or, "Where did you shop? Crummy department stores?"
Why do we have to wear name-brand clothes, Lord?
What's wrong with plain jeans and tops?
And what's so great about little shops
    where prices are so high?
Why are little stores "in"?
Most of the time I don't say anything
    when the kids start to talk like this.
Once I tried saying,
    "Clothes aren't the person.
    It's the person that's important, not the clothes."
Sharon wheeled around and said, "Oh, *I'm sorry*,"
    in that sarcastic way
    that makes me feel so low.
So I just shut up.
Not much use saying anything, is there, Lord?
Guess I'll just have to wait for them to grow up.

Let's Talk

Do the kids at school talk clothes a lot?
What is "in" just now?
If you don't wear the latest or best, what do they say?
How do you feel then?
Did Mom ever experience this when she was young?
How did she feel?
What did she do?
Does she have remarks made to her even now?
When we say a person is well groomed, what do we mean?

It Helps to Remember

Being well groomed helps us feel good about ourselves. But being well groomed does not mean we constantly have to buy new outfits to keep up with trends. If we are Christians we are careful how we spend our money. We believe there are better ways to use our money than to buy lots and lots of clothes. One good rule to remember is to dress so we do not call attention to ourselves yet look attractive. The real "me" inside of my clothes *is* the most important me.

Verses to Remember

Jesus said, "Do not be anxious about your life, what you shall eat or what you shall drink, nor about your body, what you shall put on. Is not life more than food, and the body more than clothing? . . . But seek first his [God's] kingdom and his righteousness, and all these things shall be yours as well" (Matt. 6:25-33).

55

Mindy Listens

My friend Mindy doesn't talk much,
    but she sure knows how to listen!
I was telling her about the boy down the street
    who always teases me.
Yesterday he grabbed my bike away from me
    and wouldn't give it back.
We were fighting,
    and I was trying to pull it away from him,

and all of a sudden he let go
and pushed me into our neighbor's pansy bed.
Was our neighbor mad when she saw all those crushed pansies!
"So what did you do?" Mindy asked.
"I said I'd buy some new plants and plant them."
"And did she cool off then?" Mindy asked.
"Not really," I said.
"So?" Mindy questioned.
"I felt like crying. I felt so bad.
    I just hung my head and stood there."
"I'm sorry," Mindy said.
    "Did she forgive you then?"
"I don't know," I said.
    "She just grumped and said if kids weren't so careless,
        they wouldn't get into trouble.
    I still feel bad,
        but I don't know what to do."
"I can understand how you feel," Mindy said.
The pansies are still crushed, Lord,
    but since I talked to Mindy and she listened and cared,
    my heart doesn't feel quite as sad as it did.
Maybe we can fix up the pansies too.
And thank You, Jesus, for a friend like Mindy
    who both listens
    and cares.

Let's Talk

How do you know somebody is really listening to you?

Who do you know who is a good listener?

When you spend time with this person, how do you feel?

How do you feel when you try to tell someone something and that person keeps interrupting you or starts to tell you to do something or says, "Mmm," or "Uh, huh," but you know they're not really listening?

When Job prayed, what did he ask God to do? (Job 13:17).

Who is our best listener?

Have you tried telling Him your troubles and joys?

Role play the part of a poor listener and a good listener. Ask

Mother or Dad to tell you something that concerned them or brought them joy. As they tell about it, first act out the part of a poor listener. Then act out the part of a good listener.

It Helps to Remember

Good friends listen. They stop what they are doing, if this is at all possible, and look at the person talking and listen. If they are sitting, they may lean forward. They answer in such a way that the one talking knows he or she is being heard.

A good listener cares about the one who is talking. A good listener tells the other person that he or she cares.

Just listening to a person and loving that person can help that person.

Verses to Remember

"Give ear to my words, O Lord;
. . . hearken to the sound of my cry,
my King and my God,
    for to thee do I pray" (Ps. 5:1, 2).

"But I call upon God;
    and the Lord will save me.
Evening and morning and at noon
    I utter my complaint and moan,
    and he will hear my voice" (Ps. 55:16, 17).

"The Lord hears when I call to him" (Ps. 4:3).

56

I Lost My Home, Lord

It's so hard, Lord.
It was tough having Mom and Dad divorce,
  especially because I still can't figure out why they did.
They never shouted or screamed or yelled at each other
  like some of my friends' parents do.
Mom said they just didn't love each other anymore.
That scares me.
Will they stop loving us, too? I wonder.
Mom says no,
  but I can't figure out the difference.
And then, dear Lord,
  I lost my home too.
Mom and Dad sold our home,
  and I shuffle back and forth between their apartments.
I'm not sure where home is anymore.
Why couldn't we at least have kept our home?
I could have stayed there for always,
  and Mom and Dad could have moved in and out,
  though that would have seemed strange too.
But the way it is now, Lord,
  I lost my home,
  and my neighborhood,
  and my playmates,
  and the park where we used to play,
  and the ice-cream parlor where we used to go for cones.
I'm so mixed up, Lord,
  and so sad.

Let's Talk

Why do people divorce?

Why did Mom and Dad divorce?

What difficult decisions do parents have to make when they divorce?

Why did Mom and Dad make the decisions they did?

How can children be sure that their mom and dad will continue to love them?

It Helps to Remember

Divorce is painful for everyone. If divorce takes place, remember that the problems can be worked out. When they are worked out carefully, children can know security and love and still feel they belong and they can even be happy.

Verses to Remember

"Cast all your anxieties on him, for he cares about you" (1 Pet. 5:7).

"My God will supply every need of yours according to his riches in glory in Christ Jesus" (Phil. 4:19).

57

When Mom and Dad Disagree

Mom and Dad fought again last night, Lord.
Their voices got so loud.
"You think you're always right," Mom said.
"Well, I am, aren't I?" Dad said.
"You are?" Mom shouted. "How about. . . ?"
And that started it.
Sherri and I crept back to my room.
We shut the door and sat down on my bed.
"Wow!" Sherri said.
"Midge's mother and dad got a divorce last week," I said.
Sherri nodded.
"Brian says his folks are separated."
We sat quietly for a while, and then Sherri said,
"Listen. They're still going at it."
"Do you suppose our parents will ever get a divorce?"
"I sure wonder sometimes, don't you?"
"I do. It happens so often.
    And with people you'd never dream would."
"I know. Even our pastor."
"I cried when I heard about that."
"I did too, only I didn't tell anyone.
    . . . Their voices are getting louder."
"Wonder how long it'll go on."
"And will they make up in the end?"
"Or go into a deep freeze?"
"I hate it when they do that."
"Me too."
"My stomach hurts."

"My eyes burn."
"Wish there was something we could do."
"But what?"

Let's Talk

Do you ever fight with your sisters or brothers?
How do you settle things?
Do Mom and Dad fight? Only once in a while, or often?
What do they fight about?
How do they settle their fights?
Can friendships become stronger after fights or are they weakened? Talk about this.
How can loud, noisy fights be avoided?

It Helps to Remember

All of us have disagreements from time to time and may have trouble getting along with each other. It's best to settle disagreements when we can talk and think calmly. Never try to settle a disagreement while you are still upset . . . it will surely end in an explosion. If it does lead to an angry confrontation, those who fight need to forgive each other.

Fighting is destructive both for those who are involved and for those who have to listen to it. We need to be sensitive to the dangers of both.

Verses to Remember

"Let us then pursue what makes for peace and for mutual upbuilding" (Rom. 14:19).

"He who forgives an offense seeks love" (Prov. 17:9).

58

Dad Says I'm Important to Him

Dad says I'm important to him.
He says he looks forward every night to coming home
    and seeing me.
He says he feels proud when I hit a home run,
    but he feels even prouder when our team loses,
    and I smile and congratulate the other team.
He says I bring meaning to his life,
    that because I'm here
    he goes off to work early every morning
        whistling.
He says he comes into my room before he goes to bed
    and looks at me sleeping
    and thanks God for me,
    and says a little prayer for me.
Wow! when I think about all this,
    that I'm so important to Dad,
    it makes me happy all over.
It helps make up for not having a mother to live with.
I feel so loved by my dad,
    and I'm so glad I'm important to him.
Dear God, help me to never disappoint my dad
    who believes in me so much.

Let's Talk

Who are the important people in your life?

What makes them important?

Who are the important people in your dad's life? In your mother's life? In your sisters and brothers' lives? Why?

How do we know we are important to God?

What did He do and what does He continue to do to show that we are important to Him?

Have you ever said to your friends, "Your friendship is important to me"? How do you think this would make them feel?

It Helps to Remember

We are important to many people, but no one in the whole wide world loves us or cares about us as much as God does. We are very important to Him. If no one else seems to care about us, God does.

When someone tells us we are important to him or her, it makes us want to be better people than ever. We don't want to disappoint them.

A Verse to Remember

"He who did not spare his own Son but gave him up for us all, will he not also give us all things with him?" (Rom. 8:32).

59

Stepparents

Mom's mad at me because I don't like my new stepdad.
I can't help how I feel about him.
I love my real dad
    and miss him.
My stepdad's just not the same.
He fusses over me.
Why doesn't he just leave me alone?
And I get such funny feelings
    when I see him kissing Mom
    and calling her his sweetheart.
I feel angry, Lord.
It doesn't seem right!
"Can't you see how wonderful he is?" Mom asks.
When I say,
    "But I love my real dad,
    and I want you kissing him,"
she says,
    "Please don't talk like that.
    And please don't talk about your dad
    in front of your new dad.
    It makes him feel strange."
Doesn't she think it's strange
    for me to have another dad?
And if I can't talk about my real dad . . .
    Oh, why did this have to happen to me, Lord?

Let's Talk

How do you feel about your new stepparent?
What makes it difficult to get used to him or her?

What could be done that would help you?

Now ask your new stepparent what it is like to have stepchildren. What brings joy? What is difficult?

What would help?

It Helps to Remember

Learning to know and love new stepparents or stepchildren is a heavy assignment for anyone. At least to begin with stepparents and stepchildren may not feel love for each other. But they can respect, be courteous to and try to help each other. Praying for each other will help too.

Verses to Remember

"Outdo one another in showing honor" (Rom. 12:10).

"Be glad for all God is planning for you. Be patient in trouble and prayerful always" (Rom. 12:12, TLB).

60

It Helps When Someone Shares Your Disappointment

Lord, You know how badly I wanted to be a banner-carrier.
I've been telling You.
But You know too what happened.
Julie got to be one, but I didn't.
"You're too short," our instructor said,
    when she lined us up.
"You're too short."
Just that.
And I was disqualified.
I don't think the teacher gave another thought to me
    or how much I had wanted to be part of the group.
I would have been at every practice.
I would have worked hard.

We had orchestra practice afterward.
I put my head behind my cello and cried.
And then I came home and cried some more.
Mom came into my room.
She sat on the floor by my bed in the dark
    and rubbed my back.
"I'm so sorry!" she said.
    "I know you're feeling really bad."
After a long time she said,
    "Maybe next year you'll be tall enough."

I'm not sure I will be,
    but just having Mom sit with me helped.

The next day when Julie called
    to say how sorry she was I didn't make it,
    I was able to say,
    "Not everyone could be chosen.
    There were others, too, who didn't make it.
    It's all right, Julie.
    I'll still go to all the games
        and yell my head off
        when the cheerleaders lead us."
I mean it too, Lord.
But it was having someone like Mom
    who cared how I felt
    that helped me to be able to say this
    and feel good about saying it.
Thank You, Lord, for a mom who feels with me.

Let's Talk

Do you have a friend who feels with you, who is happy when you are happy and sad when you are sad?

How does your friend let you know how he or she feels?

How do you feel when your friend supports you in this way?

Can you think of some time when a friend of yours got hurt or lost something or had something important to him or her broken?

How did your friend feel?

What did you say or do?

Can your parents or the adults in your group think of some time when a friend of theirs got into trouble or got angry about something?

What did your parents or the adults in your group do to help?

Can they think of some time when someone helped them in this way? How did they feel?

Read Mark 2:1-5. How did the friends of the paralytic show that they cared for him and felt for him?

It Helps to Remember

Learning how to feel with other people and letting them know how we feel is important if we are going to have a happy family and true friends.

A Verse to Remember

"Bear one another's burdens, and so fulfil the law of Christ" (Gal. 6:2).